# MAGICAL MOMENTS

"During the time when I was doing EEG analyses for Deborah's scientific study I read her book, trying to 'get in touch' with her ideas. I had an amazing 'spiritual-scientific' experience. In a dream I saw the meaning of brain rhythm changes when applying Deborah's approach, seen from the point of view of analytic psychology. Only profound, true ideas could provoke deep insight in other persons, and this is the wonderful 'hidden' effect of Deborah's book."

**—Svetla Velikova, MD, PhD**

"The training and techniques described in this book give me more presence of mind during my day, and within myself. They give me more energy, composure and focus, improving my ability to be pleasant when meeting others in my role as a physician as well as in my private life. In short, this training enriches my experience of life."

**—Dorthe Huse, MD**

"The simple yet powerful techniques described in this book have largely improved my life quality, and gave the strength needed to actively go for and achieve goals in my personal life as well as within business. Less stress, improved health, achieved goals and better relations to family, friends and colleagues are just a few of the results after using the techniques. I highly recommended not only reading, but actively including the contents of this book as a part of your life. I also understand that the 'magic' in my life is created by me and not by others. You will treasure it!"

**—Yngve Fahre**, Managing Director

"The mental exercises and techniques described in this book have helped me to improve relationships in my private life and in business, for example during contract negotiations. They have also enabled me to create even more smooth flow in my life than I had already. I now know that it's possible to help myself and others by using my thoughts creatively."

**—Gregers Gram Rygg Sr.**, mechanical engineer,
Senior Proposal Manager

"Being a natural skeptic makes self help built on science and hard facts a dream come true. The sense of control I feel after reading this helps take the stress and annoyance out of everyday life. And it didn't just give me all the power I could ever need—it made a huge difference to my family and my relationships when I understood what love and forgiveness really means. Read it, just do it and you'll never go back."

**—Helene Fahre**

"Many thanks for giving us unique tools and beautiful inspiration in a fantastic book that touched my heart. I see new aspects of the book every time I read it, and this gives me growth, inspiration and courage to continue on my own path. This book is a TREASURE that I'd like to give to EVERYONE."

**—Gerd Heradstveit Steinskog**

"If it hadn't been for Deborah Borgen and her teachings I wouldn't be alive now. This has truly saved my life! In addition, it's good to have tools that help me to change and transform trauma that I've experienced."

**—Wenche Karlsen**

"This is a 'must have' book! It tells you step-by-step how you can succeed in life, no matter where in life you are or what you wish to change. I've used these methods/tools since I learned about them, and have achieved results that I never could have dreamed of. I warmly recommend this book, no matter who you are or what you do!!!"

**—Torill Margrethe Stenli**

"I believe that everyone, deep inside, wants something more out of life. This book gives you understanding and the tools to bring that about!"

**—Hergunn Lund**

# MAGICAL MOMENTS

*Discover How to Easily Create*
*More in Your Daily Life*

## DEBORAH BORGEN

### WITH KIM BJØRNQVIST

NEW YORK

# MAGICAL MOMENTS
*Discover How to Easily Create More in Your Daily Life*

Originally published in Norwegian (2011) by Gyldendal Norsk Forlag AS ISBN 978-82-05-40843-2

ISBN 978-1-61448-803-3 paperback
ISBN 978-1-61448-804-0 eBook
Library of Congress Control Number:

Morgan James Publishing
The Entrepreneurial Publisher
5 Penn Plaza, 23rd Floor,
New York City, New York 10001
(212) 655-5470 office • (516) 908-4496 fax
www.MorganJamesPublishing.com

**Cover Design by:**
Rachel Lopez
www.r2cdesign.com

**Interior Design by:**
Bonnie Bushman
bonnie@caboodlegraphics.com

In an effort to support local communities, raise awareness and funds, Morgan James Publishing donates a percentage of all book sales for the life of each book to Habitat for Humanity Peninsula and Greater Williamsburg.

Get involved today, visit
www.MorganJamesBuilds.com.

**Habitat**
**for Humanity**
Peninsula and
Greater Williamsburg
Building Partner

# Contents

# *Preface*

In this book I would like to share with you the understanding and insight that I have gained from my own development and research, that have helped me to feel like a complete person, happy in my daily life even when I am surrounded by storms and chaos.

I know that you—no matter who you are—have the same possibilities that I have. We are all unique, but we also have much in common—including enormous, undreamed of possibilities. I didn't learn anything about these possibilities at home, at school or elsewhere. I've promised myself to use the rest of my life to communicate my insight to as many as possible. Then we cannot say "we didn't know," but rather be free to choose what we want and what is in accordance with our dreams and goals.

Everything that I write in this book is based on this insight. When you read the stories written by course participants, you will see that they use my techniques for very diverse goals—everything from great changes in lifestyle to small everyday matters—and what they all have in common is that they have taken control of their own lives in a new way.

This is no doubt what a magical daily life is about.

*Deborah*

# *Acknowledgements*

First of all I would like to thank Gyldendal Forlag, my Norwegian publisher, for believing in me and my work. That has opened new doors and helped me to reach out in the world with my work. Then I especially thank Michael Ebeling, who took the time and trouble to introduce me and my book to David Hancock at Morgan James Publishing. My sincere thanks goes to David Hancock and the team at Morgan James Publishing for recognizing the potential of this book and helping to present it worldwide. It has truly been a pleasure to work with the friendly, supportive and efficient Morgan James team. One of my dreams has come true.

Heartfelt thanks go also to Maryanne Rygg for her time and dedication in translating this book and other parts of my work to English.

I would also like to thank my loyal friends and colleagues at Unique Mind ESP, especially Børre, Toril and Marianne for sticking by my side, believing in me, helping and supporting me in every way for thirteen years so far.

I owe thanks also to my parents and siblings, who have been my greatest teachers, as well as to all who I have encountered on my way through life who have deeply challenged me so that I could become the person I now am.

The powerful stories and examples from course participants contained in this book impress me now as much as they did the first time I heard them. I would like to thank all of those who dared to share their experiences in such an open-hearted manner.

Last but far from least, I owe great thanks to my co-author and sparring partner, Kim Bjørnqvist. This book would not have been the same at all without the many hours he spent raising questions and looking for answers.

*Deborah Borgen*

# Kim tells about meeting Deborah

In 2001 I was the Director of Entertainment for *Nordisk Film*, a company that produces movies and TV-shows.

Our Danish sister company had produced a very successful TV-series called "Sensing Murder." The idea was to let people who claimed to be clairvoyant look into unsolved murder cases.

After only six episodes of the Danish series were aired, *TVNorge* decided to produce a Norwegian version and I was to be the executive producer for the Norwegian series.

I had of course seen the Danish program and was fascinated by what the clairvoyants found, although I didn't really believe it. I looked at it basically as a rather strange phenomenon, and most of all as brilliant TV.

The first step in the process was to find Norwegian clairvoyants, but we didn't even know if there were any. Just to be on the safe side we had an agreement with our Danish colleagues to use theirs if we didn't find anyone.

As the producer responsible for results, it was my job to start the process. I made some inquiries and found something called *Norsk Parapsykologisk Forening* (Norwegian association for parapsychology). I phoned them and told them about the planned TV-series, and asked if they knew anyone who was so-called "clairvoyant." He thought for a while before answering: "There was one up in Hallingdal Valley, but he is unfortunately dead." I almost reached for the phone to call Denmark.

However, when we got more people involved and explored the matter more thoroughly, it turned out that there were a number of Norwegians that had such abilities and who were willing to try.

"Sensing Murder" was a great success for *TVNorge* for three seasons. The only reason that we stopped was that we ran out of unsolved cases. Whether the reason is the relatively non-violent population in Norway or the superior performance of Norwegian police investigations, is something that I don't want to speculate about.

Nonetheless, this TV-series caused all who worked on it to think about what actually was behind the often remarkable results that our clairvoyants revealed.

Something that fascinated me—in addition to their abilities—was that they seldom chose the obvious paths. For example: If a woman was murdered, the police always started by investigating the closest family members, because experience shows that the murderer quite often is found among them. Our clairvoyants never did that. They could suddenly start talking about a one-armed German or a satanic ritual murder, even when none of the "facts" in the case were even close to pointing in that direction. The clairvoyants therefore needed to rely on their own abilities.

When we contacted Deborah Borgen she was already well established with her courses, and was therefore one of those who had most to lose by participating on TV, if she did not give a credible performance. Deborah was at first skeptical of the program, as she did not consider herself to be clairvoyant. The point of her courses was, to the contrary, that everyone has gut feelings and this is something that is quite natural. Her curiosity and innate urge to try out new things led Deborah to agree to participate anyway.

Deborah turned out to be one of those who found places and facts that there were absolutely no rational explanations for.

Examples are abundant, but one of the most remarkable was a murder at a place called Rena, far out in the country. The victim was found in a large forest, leaning against a tree trunk.

We drove Deborah to a parking spot about 2.5 km from the crime scene. She was surrounded by forest on all sides and received no hint about which direction to take, but she immediately started out in the right direction. With the camera crew tagging along behind her, and after a long and strenuous hike in the impenetrable forest, she walked right up to the exact tree—among a million others—and said: "This is where he was found."

A couple of years later I sat and discussed paranormal phenomena with Malcolm Alsop, one of the most experienced idea developers in English TV, who was at the time associated with a Dutch/English production company that *Nordisk Film* cooperated with. He was also fascinated by "Sensing Murder." We started discussing ideas related to that theme, and how we could design a concept for a program with a neutral starting point, where we could test the clairvoyants under controlled circumstances. This was about the time when the Idol concept had started to successfully sweep over the globe.

Our conversation suddenly came to a halt and we almost simultaneously exclaimed: "Psychic Idol!" That was the start of the project called "Psychic Challenge" that has at present been aired in 19 countries including the USA and the UK.

The concept may be summarized as follows: Some people are claimed to have clairvoyant abilities. In order to investigate this and give the TV audience an opportunity to draw their own conclusions, we gather 12 of them. In each weekly program they are given challenges that test their abilities. While the clairvoyants are working to solve their challenges, they are supervised by a neutral and a skeptical observer, to ensure that there is no cheating.

In working out the details for the series it was natural to include a clairvoyant who could explain more to us about how these abilities function and what the persons who have developed these abilities are able to do, or not able to do.

It was natural for me to contact Deborah, because she was the one who, in my opinion, was most deliberately conscious of her abilities, and who was also most curious to find out more about how they worked and what the limits were. As usual she answered that this was something she had never done before, so she would like to do it.

I'll never forget our first meeting, at my office. At that point I was still very unsure about these things—clairvoyance, sixth sense, ESP (extra sensory perception) or whatever one might call it—and how it all worked.

I began by asking Deborah about how she can say something about a person simply by holding an object belonging to that person. This was something that she and the other clairvoyants who participated in "Sensing Murder" did regularly. She explained: "By having an intention and using my ESP sense, I may receive information that is stored in the object, information that came from the person who had used it or owned it."

"OK, but if all objects contain information, what does this tell you?" I asked as I gave her my coffee cup, a metal cup with a black plastic handle that may be bought in just about any gas station in Norway.

I saw that Deborah was somewhat startled, but she took the cup without saying anything. Her fingers stroked lightly over the surface of the cup, while she closed her eyes. Without opening her eyes, she said that she saw a small boy, about seven or eight years old, with blond hair. "He's wearing blue striped shorts and a T-shirt with blue dots. He's given this to you as a gift." I felt the hairs rising on my lower arms while I picked up the phone and called my wife to ask her what our son was wearing that day. She answered that he had gone to school that day in shorts with blue stripes and a shirt with blue dots. He had just turned eight, and he had given the cup to me for my birthday.

From that instant I stopped wondering whether there really were people who are clairvoyant, and became more concerned about how these abilities function and what they can be used for.

This was the beginning of our work together, which resulted in "Psychic Challenge" being aired by Channel Five in England, as the first of 19 countries.

Deborah made it clear right from the start that these abilities are natural and certain, something that everyone has and can develop. Deborah seemed to me to be a strong opponent of false mysticism or hysterical ego-massage practiced by many of those who call themselves clairvoyant. This was sometimes hard to swallow for those who didn't know her well. One sort of expects that "clairvoyants" are to behave in a certain manner and usually be somewhat mystical.

Deborah is just the opposite—down-to-earth and sensible—and she is firmly of the opinion that we all have these abilities and that they can be developed to an almost unlimited degree. I have never looked upon myself as being especially down-to-earth. To the contrary, I am rather marked by a childhood during the 1960s, with solid influence from hippie philosophy.

On the other hand, I have worked for my entire adult life as a businessman, have run my own companies and have worked in large, international companies without having any problem following the rules of play in that environment. After meeting Deborah, I felt an urge to start exploring the part of myself that lies below the surface.

It started when Deborah and I sat on a plane to London and just chatted. At the time I was very overweight. To put it plainly: I was too fat.

We talked about that, and I complained that I had tried every weight-loss plan and none had a lasting effect.

"Have you found the real reason for weighing too much?" asked Deborah. "That's not difficult," I answered. "Too much food and too little exercise." Deborah smiled knowingly and said: "I think it's about time for you to participate in one of my courses."

A few days later my wife and I sat on our chairs in a large conference hall in Oslo, together with about two hundred other people. I thought desperately to myself: "Help, we're now going to sit here for 20 hours and just listen to Deborah?"

On Sunday evening we looked at each other and quickly agreed that we hadn't had such an enjoyable weekend for a long time. Just sitting, relaxing, meditating and going within, is a pleasure that most of us don't allow ourselves in our busy lives.

That was basically how I experienced my first course. No earthshaking aha-experiences. No burning bush or hallelujah shouts. But I started using the techniques I had learned. Then came the changes. Slowly, my life began to flow more smoothly. Not from one day to the next, but gradually the pieces of my life came together.

And the overweight? After some serious dialogue with myself in The Creative Corner, I found the answer that Deborah had asked about on the plane to London. I understood why I was fat. It had nothing to do with what was outside of me, but a lot to do with what was within.

I went to a doctor who recommended a Grete Roede course for weight control that turned out to be perfect for me. To make a long story short: One year later I had lost 22.5 kilos and written a book (*Gutta på kur*, meaning "Boys on Cure," a pun relating to a famous Norwegian TV-series, "Boys on Tour") together with my good friend Finn Bjelke who accompanied me and lost about the same amount of weight.

So far I've maintained that weight without any problems. I'm not as slim as a model, but I'm healthy and I enjoy good food and wine as I always have!

I've also stopped running to catch a trolley or bus. I often use public transportation, and before the course I was often stressed and ran after the trolley or bus, panting for breath and swearing when I didn't reach it in time.

Thanks to Deborah's course I remember to hold a positive focus before leaving home or work on my way to the subway. This has become automatic—I don't sit massaging my temples and envisioning gray subway cars. Sometimes I calmly wait a little before going out the door. Other times I quickly pack my things and hurry off to the stop.

With my hand on my heart I swear: I seldom wait more than two or three minutes at the stop any more, and most often the trolley or bus arrives at the stop at the same time that I do.

I no longer "hate" anything either. I was previously very busy judging other people, their behavior, their efforts, etc. Now I'm most concerned about how I myself can make the best possible effort and what I can do to make the world a little better.

Now it might sound like I'm Saint Francis of Assisi, but I absolutely do not think of myself as any better, more worthy or more thoughtful than others. I've just become more aware of my own place in the world and I concentrate on that—and not on all the others.

Many people think that religious viewpoints and interpretations are involved in self-development of the type we describe in this book. I recommend keeping an open mind. The principles and techniques that are described here work equally well for those who are religious, those who are atheists, and just as well for Buddhists as for Hindus.

# Deborah's path and development

(Much of this book is written as a conversation between Deborah Borgen and Kim Bjørnqvist. When Kim poses a question or comments, the text appears in italics. Deborah's answers appear as normal text.)

*Who are you really, Deborah?*

Who am I? That's something I work on every day by going within. My conscious self-development started in 1986. At the time I was a stressed business executive and never had enough time. I felt more and more anxiety, and collapsing was unavoidable. I can see that now, looking back with the insight I have gained about humans and how you and I function.

*How did your self-development start?*

You might say that I was forced to make changes in my life, and I was lucky to have two choices. I could choose death by continuing as I had been doing, or I could choose to look for solutions that helped me to understand how I could live and have a good life. Due to my children the choice was clear, but it still wasn't easy. My conscious search for a good life started there.

My Dad was an alcoholic. He was well-meaning, but life was unstable as a child of an alcoholic, and led to some experiences that made their mark on my childhood and youth. I quickly learned to interpret moods—will this be a good or a difficult day? I began to develop my ESP sense to be able to feel and perceive moods and atmospheres.

While growing up I had many traumatic experiences. I was raped first when I was eleven by one man, and then when I was about thirteen I was repeatedly sexually abused by a doctor that my parents trusted. He gave them the impression that he was taking care of me by allowing me to live with his own family for a while after I had run away from home, but this sly man had other intentions. He was married and had two children, and it is difficult to understand such behavior.

*Do you hate him today?*

"I don't," said Deborah while smiling. "You see, I have learned about forgiveness. I've forgiven the person, but not the deed."

*But how did you manage to live with that before you had found all your tools?*

When I was 25 years old I had been married twice and had three children. By then I'd had more than enough. I couldn't cope with life any longer. Like many others I was raised to suppress my feelings, to keep painful things to myself. But my emotions churned within me. I became seriously ill. The experience that started the whole process was quite peculiar and exciting.

My third child, my daughter, was born by Caesarean operation (C-section). I was to be put under general anesthesia, but I was lying there still fully awake when I heard the doctor say: "Now she is ready." But I wasn't, and there I was panic-stricken with a paralyzed body when I felt them starting to cut. I tried to blink my eyelids and move my arms, but I couldn't move a muscle. When they began to cut I felt a piercing pain, but then the pain suddenly disappeared and I was "outside of my body."

I could see that they were operating. I heard the doctors talk about everyday things like where they were going for vacation. When I talked with the chief physician after the operation and told him what I had experienced, he confirmed what I recalled about their conversation. He also said that some people experience this, but doctors cannot explain what had happened.

It was fascinating. I found out that body and thoughts do not always need to be in the same place.

Fascinating or not, I became seriously ill and developed bulimia, which had nothing to do with getting slim, my body, or my weight. My body was just reacting to my lack of an outlet for my feelings.

It was truly hellish. I finally became so thin and sick that I had to admit myself to an institution with the help of a lawyer, due to my great loss of weight and liquids. At the time there was little knowledge in this area, and they did not want to admit me.

Not long after that I admitted myself to a closed ward—I was so desperate. There must be someone who could help me? I was released a few days later with a remark from the chief physician that I "had better understanding of myself than they did."

A therapist who practiced kinesthetic medicine noticed my story, and he believed he could help me. He pointed out how much negativity I had within me. I felt insulted. I was a typical "yes" person, a good girl who felt that I always focused on the positive.

That was the first step of my self-development. I have now spent almost 27 years asking "why is this so?" "how does this work?" and many other questions.

*I think that many who find themselves in difficult situations despair because they don't know where to start. What did you do?*

As I said, the therapist who practiced kinesthetic medicine was the first person I talked to about these things. He told me that I had an excess of negative thoughts and episodes in my life. He said that when there is too much negativity in relation to the positive, we get sick. Well, that made me curious and interested in what we think about and what we store in our subconscious mind. I worked diligently with myself to change my thoughts and attitudes. It became so interesting that I dared for the first time to talk about this theme in an oral exam in business English at college. My examiners found it very interesting, and their response helped me to seriously consider sharing my experience with others in the form of lectures and courses.

*But you wanted to continue your self-development?*

Yes. At the same time that I met the therapist I mentioned, I read a self-development book for the first time: *Stop Worrying and Start Living* by Dale Carnegie. (The Norwegian title translates to: *Stop Complaining and Start Living*). That is exactly where I was; I complained more than I lived, so this book was an eye-opener for me. I had, however, at least started changing negative thoughts and attitudes in my life. I learned that it was very difficult to make lasting changes.

*What do you think was the reason for the lack of lasting changes, Deborah?*

That is a question that I pondered about quite a lot. I was frustrated because I had no tools to help me, and I was also impatient. I wanted instant changes. The book by Carnegie inspired me to create an inner room for myself—inside me—where I could philosophize and lay the groundwork for a happy life. A happy life was a remote dream for me at the time, but somewhere within myself I did believe that all humans have the same possibilities to find a good life. My grandmother taught me that, and I trusted her.

*How important is that belief?*

Every self-development begins with a decision to change something in your life, and you must believe that it's possible. I made use of my inner room every day. There I could talk to myself or find a "partner" to discuss things with. I've always been curious, but I also need to find and understand explanations that make sense and seem logical. I can use hours, days, months or years, as long as I finally understand. Every evening before going to sleep I wrote down the challenges I had encountered during the day in a journal, and prepared the next day with the best solutions that I could imagine.

*I begin to recognize elements from your course!*

That's right, and it's important for me that I've already used the techniques I recommend to others, and found that they work.

After working on my own for a while, I found a course about the methods taught by José Silva. This was a confirmation for me that the thoughts I had been thinking and the direction I was going in, were also being studied by others. I became fascinated by his philosophy that we are here on Earth to make it better by using more creativity and finding better solutions for the whole; not just being concerned about ourselves and our ego. José Silva made me curious about our brainwave frequencies. He believed that by lowering the frequencies we can attain a state of greater calmness and balance. There wasn't much research available at the time, so I decided that one of my goals was that I would one day contribute to research in this area.

*Why are you so interested in research and facts? Isn't self-development about feelings and intuition?*

I am a person who cannot just accept everything without evidence. I therefore decided to see if I could, by lowering my brainwave frequencies, influence the health of others. I worked for five years documenting this. Some call it healing, and there are many myths surrounding this.

People came to me and thought I was special, since I could positively influence the health and psyche of others. Some began to look suspiciously at me and say: "Are you carrying on with those alternative things, or what?" I don't think there is anything alternative about using both brain hemispheres, and that is what I was doing.

While in my inner room I also found a way to remove negative episodes and experiences from my subconscious, so that I could make the lasting changes I had longed for.

*Deborah, this definitely sounds mystical.*

You think so? Yes, some people called me a witch, others just shook their heads, and I thought it was sad that they weren't interested in hearing about getting less stressed, lowering brainwave frequencies and finding a better life. All that I could do was to work on my own feelings and keep dreaming that I would one day show that I am completely normal and that everyone has the same possibility to help others in this way.

I have now been able to prove this, and a large pilot study that will lead to more research was completed in January 2011.

The burning desire that I had about helping others find new insight and development, led me to work with José Silvas methods for ten years, using various lectures and courses. I also met him in person, and he had the same burning desire to share his insight. He became, in addition to Dale Carnegie and Mother Teresa, a source of inspiration and a mentor that I could "talk to" in my inner room. In my inner room I can talk with whoever I like, be they living or dead.

*You don't make it easy for yourself by saying such things?*

No, I don't always chose the easiest way to reach my goal, but clearly the one that teaches me the most. Because I have been near death three times in my life and been opened for lower brainwave frequencies, I was somewhat naive, to put it that way.

I really believed that other people wanted the same as I did: to work for better solutions. I had opened up so much along the way that I had no filter, so when envious attitudes hit me I was astonished. I couldn't believe my own eyes when I found how malicious people can be to each other. The time had come to go even deeper within myself than I had earlier.

I continued to study humans through my own inner work. I also continued to work to prove that humans have a source of inner wisdom that they may gain access to by using the whole brain and thereby operating at lower brainwave frequencies. I learned early in life to be sensitive to moods and to read situations in order to avoid conflict, and my gut feelings developed even more due to additional difficult situations.

*And along that path, we met!*

Yes, in 2002 I was contacted by *Nordisk Film*. Your company was preparing to produce a TV-program where clairvoyants were to participate and help solve some yet unsolved murder mysteries. I had some prejudices at the time. I had learned that psychics were people who thought they had some special gift, and that they pestered the police with phone calls. I didn't want to give an impression of being one of those "psychics" and was at first negative to the whole idea.

*You weren't alone. There were many prejudices that arose to the surface when the TV-series was aired.*

I didn't consider myself to be clairvoyant and hadn't worked in that way earlier, but someone who knew my work had tipped *Nordisk Film* about me. Since I had a strong desire to show that everyone has gut feelings that may be used for good purposes, I chose to meet with representatives from *Nordisk Film* to discuss the TV-series called "Sensing Murder." When I was convinced that this was a serious and respectable series, I participated for all three of the seasons it was aired.

Of course the TV-series prompted much debate for and against, and I was happy that I had my tools to help me cope. Many different words were used to describe us, and we were accused of having received information beforehand or just reading the thoughts of others. I was able to clearly disprove this in an episode that took place in a huge forest. The camera crew thought that we were lost, but I found exactly the place where the murder victim had been found, and I easily found my way back as well.

Enhanced gut feelings may be used in many ways, and one of my goals is to train the police so that they strengthen their gut feelings.

*There was to be more TV?*

Yes, in 2005 *Nordisk Film* was to begin producing a Norwegian version of "The Power of Spirits," and I was again asked to participate. This time I was even more skeptical, because I don't believe in ghosts in the form that many have been taught to believe in them.

We all remember spooky stories that were told when we were young. Our imagination could run wild with us, and we had no control. We saw shadows everywhere and could incorporate all the creaking sounds into the story. One of the producers convinced me that it was important for me to participate because I would then have an opportunity to demystify these phenomena, and that was decisive for me when I agreed. I participated in two seasons.

*But is your participation in these TV-series consistent with your level-headed view of life?*

As I mentioned, I am an economist and one who needs to analyze and understand. I also need to see evidence. That was one of the reasons I agreed to participate in these programs. In one way it resulted in new insight for me about how the conscious and the subconscious minds interconnect, and that we—with lower brainwave frequencies and good balance—can gain access to a potential that we have not been able to find explanations for. It has been, and is, of utmost importance in my life to show that we have hidden abilities and can use them to create a better life.

After this phase of my life I adjusted my goals and continued my inner search for ways to proceed and methods to explain, in order to help others to be able to get in touch with their inner potential.

*And now we have come to "Psychic Challenge."*

Yes. When you contacted me in 2006 about the idea for a program about the sixth sense, I felt that could be a way to begin.

A new phase for understanding and learning had begun. I helped to create tests and try out the tests and was a mentor in the series. It was an unbelievable learning experience and was thrilling for the analytical side of myself. I remember well a producer in Netherland where I was to do some tests. He gave me a ring, and I was to find out who it belonged to. I suddenly saw, in my inner room, a woman from India with a mark on her forehead. She told me a story; that she was his wife, how they had adopted a child from India, and that she herself had died from heart disease. The man was a widower. I understand that others feel that this is not normal and is beyond comprehension. This is all the more reason for me to teach people to use their gut feelings for goal-oriented self-development for a good life, with inner balance.

*Yes, I recall the expression on his face. Not to mention a photographer who worked on the project who had explicitly expressed skepticism about everything that he could not explain. Finally one of the Dutch participants got so irritated that she went over to him, took hold of his arm and told him exactly what it looked like in his apartment, where she of course had never been. As all of the details were precisely correct, we could see that he became more and more pale. He didn't say a word the rest of the day.*

*After a few more years you launched your own self-development program in 2010?*

Yes, a program that trains us to use all of our brain in order to reach our goals and to open the possibilities that are innate in each individual.

*After our work with the program about the sixth sense, we didn't see much of each other. But in 2009 you contacted me again and we met to discuss some ideas you had. You told me of your plan for a book.*

That's right. I had written a book manuscript on my laptop. One day at an airport the laptop "accidently" fell out of my bag and the hard disk was destroyed. I had no backup of the manuscript and it was not possible to reconstruct it. I then understood that the destroyed manuscript was part of a learning process I needed to go through before the final book could come into being.

*I then heard myself say that you should just let me know if you wanted help from me. I was a little surprised to hear myself say that, because I had just written a book and definitely had no plans to write another right away!*

No, but it felt right when you said it, and before long we were underway!

*Coincidence?*

Not a chance. You know better, Deborah laughed.

# What do we mean by
# "A Magical Daily Life?"

*The title of this book is quite ambitious, Deborah, and people will interpret the word "magical" in different ways. It almost sounds like we want people to live like Harry Potter. What do you mean when you use the words "a magical daily life?"*

For me it means that I discover small things every day that make me feel fortunate, and give me a feeling of being in the right place at the right time, the sum of which gives a feeling of something magical happening. A feeling of happiness. A nice experience that illustrates this was a bus ride I had from Evenes airport to the town of Harstad in Norway. I was to give a lecture that evening. The bus was full of people who were going to attend a conference. They were very stressed, talking in their phones and with each other quite loudly. You might say that the bus was filled with stress energy. I had a window seat and looked around, quite relaxed and calm. I was unaffected by the atmosphere in the bus. I'm very happy about that, because while they were stressed, I could see the rabbit that was hopping in the snow.

I'm not talking about great miracles, but about the sum of elements that help life to flow more smoothly so that you don't just accept the struggle for existence, but feel that you are really alive!

More precisely, it's about having much more of what many people call "good luck." I prefer to call it smooth flow, simply because you experience that all areas of life flow more smoothly.

*I know the feeling, and what you are saying also appears in all of the stories that are included in this book. For me, the most important word in the title may be the word daily. I think that many, myself included, associate magic in life with nice holidays and vacations that are memorable. However, even in wealthy Norway, people have only five or six weeks of vacation, so if you feel you have a magical life only during those weeks, life becomes sad and empty. It's definitely in our daily lives that we need the many small, magical and uplifting experiences, right?*

Yes, clearly, and most of the feedback I receive is about the positive changes in daily life that people experience. Many people are not used to having so much luck and good fortune in their daily lives, or focusing on it when it happens.

Another aspect is that when you experience well being and smooth flow, you also influence those around you; there is a positive synergistic effect that spreads like rings on the water.

*Aren't you afraid that people will think that since we can use tools that help to find the right plumber, etc., then we should also be able to buy a winning lottery ticket and cash in the prize money? (Deborah looks exasperated. She's been asked that question so many times.)*

Is that so magical? Is it money that gives us magical experiences in daily life? If you're thinking that you would like to have a better place to live or a better job so the family can be better off, or something else like that, then yes, the tools can help you. These are things that you need, that are useful for you. But money in itself is not magical.

We have, in addition, stored so much within ourselves about money being the root of all evil; that money does not lead to happiness; that money isn't everything. So nothing will happen that brings us money until we transform all of those inner truths.

I also believe that it isn't easy to call upon that within ourselves that will have money for money's sake. Why would we want that? Is it to appear better than others?

In other words, if you would like to have money in order to take the family on a great vacation, so focus on the vacation and you will see that it materializes!

*But many associate money with happiness?*

Happiness is a feeling that arises from within. In order to choose happiness we must know something about how humans function and how we can maintain control of our imagination and our feelings. We can choose happiness. That is what this book is about: How may I choose happiness and experience a magical daily life?

When I read a book by Jill Bolte Taylor, *My Stroke of Insight*, I felt that she confirmed much of what I had been thinking. This American brain scientist had a hemorrhage that affected her left brain hemisphere only. In her book she tells of her recovery from a condition where only her right brain hemisphere was intact. One thing that she wrote was: An automatic response releases chemicals from the brain. It happens in less than 90 seconds. If our previous thought persists after 90 seconds, it is because we *choose* to let it continue.

I have always said that we can choose our thoughts, we just need to understand the process. When the process is such that we can choose a different thought and hold it for 90 seconds in order for the feeling to be transmitted to our bodies, then we *are* able to choose happiness.

*Before we begin to talk about how to find happiness, it would be good to define what happiness is—and what it is not. When you are without money, it's easy to believe that happiness has something to do with financial security, or even abundance. We shouldn't be arrogant by saying that being well off financially has nothing to do with happiness. Security in every area of life, also our finances, is an important factor when we describe how happy we are. But financial security alone is definitely not enough.*

*Neither are beautiful looks, for if that were the case there would not be so many actors or models who are alcoholics or addicts.*

*Good relationships, children, a job that you like—all of these are elements that may contribute to happiness, but each one is not enough by itself.*

*It's about creating the right combination?*

You might put it that way. Your definition of happiness, as well as mine, is to be in balance. Putting together a life consisting of ingredients that complement and nourish each other gives happiness.

Everyone has experienced a state of happiness, such as the spectacular moments of happiness when a child is born, when we fall in love, experience triumphs at work, and even when your team scores.

*Both of us have met challenges in life, you perhaps more than most people. How does that affect your feeling of happiness?*

I've been through many disappointments and demanding challenges that a lot of people would describe as "unhappy." Nonetheless, both you and I would answer positively if someone asked us if we were happy. It *is* possible as long as one has learned how to cope with those situations.

There are some people with terminal illness who say that they live a rich life and that they also feel happy. These people have found the key to inner wisdom.

Happiness, balance, or whatever you would like to call it, does not appear on its own, unfortunately. It requires some effort, like so much else in life.

Who wouldn't be willing to spend some time in order to find balance, smooth flow and happiness? We're not talking in terms of hours. Most people are surprised about how little time it takes.

*Do you mean that we tend to exaggerate our problems?*

Our problems tend to grow in size in our own eyes, when we don't do anything about them. They finally become so great that they seem unsolvable, and we sink into despair. Then someone comes along and makes a simple suggestion and we suddenly see a solution.

Many "unsolvable" problems may have simple solutions. We just don't see them.

*That reminds me of the story of a man who told his psychologist that he heard someone under his bed that kept him awake at night. The psychologist said that this could be cured but it was complicated, would take a long time and cost a lot of money. The man said that he would think about it.*

*Two weeks later they coincidentally bumped into each other on the street, and the psychologist asked how it was going, since he hadn't heard from his patient. "I've cured myself," said the man. "I just cut the legs off my bed!"*

That story is a good one, and illustrates how we often remove symptoms without correcting the cause that is within us. In order to achieve a magical daily life we need to do both.

# *How to use this book*

I recommend that you read through the whole book first, to get familiar with the material. If you read something that causes some reaction, take a deep breath and then go on reading. This is a part of the process of goal-oriented self-development.

When you've read the whole book, you are ready to start goal-oriented work for your conscious and deliberate self-development.

Start again with the first chapter, and this time you should read more thoroughly. Many have been taught that they should not write in a book, and that books should be handled with care. This book is meant to be used as a workbook. While reading, underline all that is important for you, make notes in the margin or use a colored marker. Learning is an active process, and notes and color make learning more fun and engaging.

Work through one chapter at a time, and when you get to a chapter with an exercise, you are to use one week on the recommended exercise.

Now you might be thinking: "Help! How long is it going to take to get through this book?" or "I just don't have time for that." These thoughts are saboteurs that are stopping by for a visit. You will become more familiar with the saboteur during weeks to come.

For best results it is important to integrate the material and new way of thinking into your consciousness.

In this way the book will be your companion for a few months, helping you on your way to conscious, deliberate and goal-oriented self-development, and will give you an understanding of how you can create a magical daily life.

When you are finished with the whole process, you might well start all over again. You will then find that you read with new eyes and notice something new. Self-development is a continual process that helps you to maintain your magical daily life.

# You have unlimited potential— and unlimited possibilities

"The intuitive mind is a sacred gift, and the rational mind a loyal servant. We have built a society that honors the servant and has forgotten the gift."
—Albert Einstein (1879–1955)

*You've made a wall chart showing the development of humans. At the very top is the word DEVELOPMENT. What do you mean by that?*

Yes, I've made the wall chart as simple as possible in order to communicate my intuitive understanding. On this chart, development means the development of human beings, the development of the brain over time as well as self-development, or own development to put it another way.

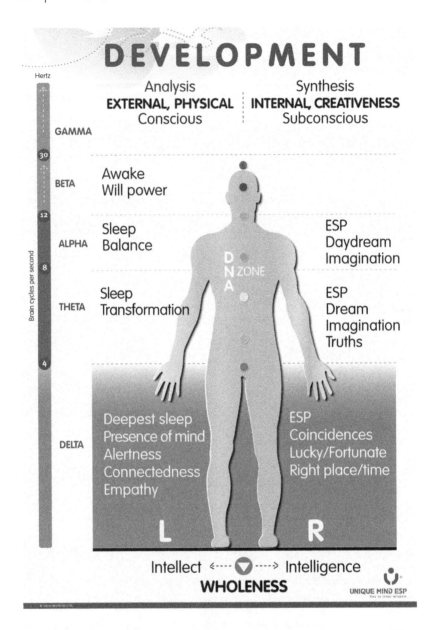

A human consists of two parts: a physical outer and a creative inner level. We have five physical senses that help us to orient ourselves in the physical world, and we have an ESP sense that helps us to orient ourselves within. The ESP sense is explained in another chapter. Everything is first created at an inner level before it appears at the physical level. An airplane, for example. Someone first got the idea at their inner creative level, and then it was built physically for all to see. All new creation happens in this way.

On the left side of the chart we find the word "conscious," and on the right side the word "subconscious." Conscious is everything we are aware of while awake, that we experience with our five physical senses, and all that we know about ourselves and others. The subconscious is all that we are not aware of while awake, and the goal is to increase access to the subconscious in order to increase our consciousness in daily life.

*Do you mean that the place called the DNA zone on the chart is the place where the subconscious becomes available to us?*

Yes, that's right, and it is in addition the area for balance, another thing that is important for me to tell you about.

*Why is that so important?*

We have two brain hemispheres that take care of different tasks, and the corpus callosum transfers information between the two hemispheres. When the lines of communication are open we are able to use all of our potential.

Dr. Roger Walcott Sperry was a neuropsychologist who was one of those awarded the 1981 Nobel Prize in medicine for his research about the two brain hemispheres, and since then more research has been done in this area.

We use our left brain hemisphere when we talk, write, solve mathematical problems, think logically and analyze. The right brain hemisphere is the center for creativity, imagination, emotions, comprehension and understanding.

On the left side of the chart we see the word "analysis." This is because our left brain hemisphere deals with analysis and examines details. When examining a forest, for example, the left brain hemisphere would see only one tree at a time. On the right side of the chart you will see the word "synthesis," which means forming a complex whole by combining. In this case, the right brain hemisphere is able to see the whole forest.

On the left side of the chart you will also find a scale showing levels of brainwave frequencies, which happens to coincide with the development of the brain by age in years. Scientists have for many years divided the frequency levels into four main groups, but now an important fifth one has been added. Depending on the level of brainwave frequencies that we have, possibilities exist that we have not earlier believed or understood. This book and the course I have designed helps people to discover for themselves what these possibilities are.

*You need to explain that more thoroughly!*

There is electrical activity in our brains that is measured by an electroencephalograph (EEG). The activity is measured in hertz, or cycles per second. Professor Emeritus in psychology, Hans Berger, was one of the first who carried out such measurements in the 1920s, so these cycles are also known as Berger rhythm.

## Briefly about the groups

**Gamma** (30–40 hertz, high Gamma 40–50 hertz) is among other things associated with a good memory and learning process. Gamma activity increases when we are under great pressure and is also associated with alertness and ingenuity.

**Beta** (12–25 hertz, high Beta 25–30 hertz) is a level that relates to the activities of the left brain hemisphere. Beta activity that is too high can lead to stress, anxiety and anger, and can cause the body to go into a state of emergency preparedness. At this level we are consciously awake and steered by our will. We are also limited by time and space.

**Alpha** (8–12 hertz) is related to light sleep and daydreaming. It is at this level that our two brain hemispheres are able to communicate.

**Theta** (4–8 hertz) is related to deeper sleep, narcosis and hypnosis. We gain access to a level where we can make lasting changes.

**Delta** (1–4 hertz) relates to deepest sleep, and at this level we gain access to a more comprehensive perspective, including empathy. A combination of Delta and Gamma frequencies gives alertness and ingenuity, sharp focus and presence of mind. Delta is also a level for connection to something greater than oneself, a solidarity.

*You often use a simple metaphor to explain this.*

Yes, I use Freud's metaphor of the mental iceberg as an illustration of the full potential we have as humans and how the conscious and the subconscious are related to each other.

An iceberg is constantly moving, and only about ten per cent of it is visible. The rest lies below the surface of the water and is the part that steers the floating iceberg. Since the iceberg is in water and water moves, this means that the lower part becomes visible at times due to the movement of waves.

If we compare this to the chart of the brain, the visible part of the iceberg would be the physical exterior, where we are awake and conscious. The brainwave frequencies would be Gamma and Beta, with the tasks of the left brain hemisphere dominating. Since the surface of the water moves up and down, we can gain access to the subconscious now and then, but it still remains a part of the subconscious. An example might be that we get an idea for a good creative solution while we are awake, without being aware that it comes from the subconscious level.

I equate the part of the iceberg that is under the surface of the water with our creative inner, the realm of sleep and the subconscious. The brainwave frequency levels here are Alpha, Theta and Delta, and the tasks of the right brain hemisphere dominate.

You will notice that on the illustration of the iceberg, the Alpha frequencies are found at the surface of the water. This is to show that Alpha frequencies make efficient cooperation between our two brain hemispheres possible, at a level where all functions are available in the physical exterior.

The Theta level gives us an opportunity to work on earlier experiences and transform all that hinders us from reaching our goals, thereby increasing our possibilities.

Delta makes it possible to reach in to the best part of ourselves, where fear goes away and empathy comes forth. The ego disappears, making way for more comprehensive thinking that best serves all parties in cooperation. Smooth flow and presence of mind are available to us and are present in our lives. As mentioned, Delta together with Gamma gives alertness and ingenuity as well as a feeling of cohesion in life.

*On your chart about development you write "intellect" to the left and "intelligence" on the right. Can you please explain that?*

For me this is an important point for comprehensive understanding. A number of years ago I read something by the German philosopher Arthur Schopenhauer. He described intellect as being related to the will and intelligence as being related to the innate potential of humans.

*So that is why you always say that none of us are born special, but that we all are unique?*

That's how I think, yes. If we operate on the lowest brainwave frequency level while awake, then we access our innate possibilities. Delta frequency level opens your "hidden" potential and your possibilities, and is the key to inner wisdom.

In the chapter about the Nightfilm technique I will explain more about what I mean by greater comprehensive thinking.

*Many who work on self-development become very self-centered and fanatical. Although much of what you talk about may sound strange and supernatural to many, you are very down-to-earth and not at all fanatical. Why is that?*

I believe in bringing the extremes into balance. Not being fanatical in any direction. Since I work as I do, I might well go around in a kind of dream bubble and float on a pink cloud, but then I would probably not communicate very well with the rest of the world.

We need to use our brain in balance. If we use one brain hemisphere too much, that would not serve us well in the long run. Think about the iceberg. If you're not in contact with your subconscious, you will be guided by what seems rational and sensible at that level. However, when using that level only, you lack a comprehensive overview.

Being in balance is of utmost importance in life. Being in balance at all times is the foundation needed in order to be a happy person. Your life cannot flow smoothly if you are not in balance.

I've thought a lot about balance in relation to work, which is a large part of our lives for most of us. Some aspects of our work are fun and interesting, while some are dull routine chores that we do because we must, or because someone tells us to. I would advise you, the reader, to look closely at what it is about your job that makes you feel happy, and what does just the opposite. Write a list of pros and cons for yourself, and if the job you have today gives a lopsided result, then sit down and think carefully about whether it is possible to change to something else that contains more elements that give happiness. It may be easier than you think. You do have a choice!

# Stress in everyday life

When people talk about positive stress, I believe they mean a good, positive flow. We will get back to that positive, smooth flow in the chapter about the Nightfilm technique.

Something that has helped me to be less stressed and find a good life, is to evaluate stress according to how my body reacts to it. I've learned to understand the conscious and the subconscious, and as I see it there is no such thing as positive stress. Stress affects the body negatively—worries, fear, negative thoughts—and it all comes from the subconscious. In the next chapter I will explain in more detail about how we are built, based on the mental vs. the physical.

*Can stress sometimes be positive—a motor?*

I know that many feel that way, but I don't completely agree. When we are under stress—in situations with great pressure—our brain operates at the level of Gamma frequencies. We may perform better for short periods, but after a length of time we become fatigued and may also feel anxiety.

That is why it's important to have strategies that help one to relax occasionally, as the exercises in this book and my courses do.

*I've worked with ideas for my whole life—in advertising, as an author, and for the past ten years with ideas for TV shows. In all of these processes I've been driven by a kind of "positive anxiety" that what I do will not be good enough, even when it's things that I've done hundreds of times before. I regard that feeling as a kind of motor that helps me to perform better and create a better product.*

There is a hairline balance here. If one lives exclusively at the pressured level of brain activity, the stress becomes negative and one becomes anxious, and that is never positive. Sooner or later one is guaranteed to hit the wall. Just consider all those who do some form of artistic work and become famous for it—how often do we not hear about nervous breakdowns, substance abuse and in the worst case, suicide? They are successful in one area, but the rest of their lives are an unhappy chaos. This is because they do not have some form of safety valve that can relieve the pressure.

However, if you manage to combine both high and low brainwave frequencies, you can perform at a high level while remaining full of energy and maintaining good health.

*That sounds like a magical daily life.*

With a laugh, Deborah said: "I call it smooth flow."

# Assignment for the week

To find a magical daily life you must get in touch with yourself again. The first step is to become less stressed.

It's important to choose times that are convenient for you, but be aware that if it "never" is convenient, your subconscious might be tricking you. You must, in fact, set aside time in order to succeed. I recommend that you use the following exercise at least once a day for a week. I also recommend that you find a place where you can sit undisturbed. If you should nonetheless be disturbed, then start the exercise again from the beginning.

Learn the steps in the exercise before you do it.

### Exercise 1: For relaxation

- Sit down and find a comfortable position with your hands resting in your lap. Close your eyes.
- Take a deep breath, and while exhaling think of the number 7 and focus your attention on your scalp.
- Let go of all stress and all worries, and feel your scalp relaxing. Give yourself plenty of time.
- Think that there is a light right above your head. You decide what this light is like. The light is to help you to relax.
- Then think that you allow the light to flow downward and spread out, covering your entire scalp.
- When your scalp feels relaxed, proceed to the number 6 and repeat as above, but with focus on your forehead. Then you continue working downward until you reach number 1.
- Number 5 is your throat. In addition, let the light spread around your neck and down to cover your shoulders, arms and hands, as well as down your back.
- Number 4 is your chest.
- Number 3 is your stomach area, between your lower ribs.
- Number 2 is your abdomen.

- Number 1 is the bottom of your torso.
- When you are finished with number 1, allow the light to flow down both of your legs simultaneously: down your thighs, knees, calves and out in both feet.
- Remain sitting for a few minutes and enjoy the feeling of complete relaxation in your entire body.

When you would like to end the session, use the method described below.

### Procedure for concluding all exercises where counting down from 7 to 1 was used

When you relax in this way, it's like being deeply asleep, and many experience discomfort from being awakened from deep sleep. To avoid discomfort it is important to follow this procedure.

### Counting out

- First, decide to end this exercise.
- Think of the number 1, then begin to carefully move your toes, then your lower legs, followed by moving your entire legs. Use a few seconds to do this.
- Think of the number 2 and begin to move your fingers, your hands and then your entire arms, while you prepare to awaken.
- Think of the number 3. Open your eyes and say to yourself: I am now wide awake and feel as if I've had a good night's sleep.

# The conscious and
# subconscious dimensions

We humans consist of two dimensions: the physical, conscious dimension, and the creative, subconscious dimension. As mentioned earlier, the physical, conscious part of us is used when we hear, smell, taste, see and touch—in other words, what we know of, and which is indisputable for many. The creative, inner subconscious is non-physical, where we use our ESP sense to perceive. We will explain more about the ESP sense in the next chapter. Your experiences, however, are based on what you have stored in your subconscious, and we haven't yet learned much about that.

*You need to explain, Deborah.*
    I'll do my best. To gain a greater understanding, we need to consider two important circumstances. One is how our thoughts affect our body and consequently also our surroundings. The other is what resides in our subconscious and directs us—the part of the iceberg that steers.

Thoughts affect the body, both conscious thoughts and all that is stored in the subconscious. What do we go around thinking in our daily lives? Many people are constantly irritated or frustrated. Notice what happens to you in such situations. You feel completely drained. When we think of nice things, the opposite is true. It can be useful to notice this, as it will confirm what we say here. In a later chapter we will describe an exercise where the goal is to become more aware of one's own thoughts and words.

However, our thoughts affect not only ourselves, but others too. There was a time when companies sent their employees on so-called "smile courses." However, it doesn't help to smile on the outside if we are radiating negative thoughts. Then the smile is false, and others register a discrepancy.

We do register that emission. Those who radiate something positive, are people who have good charisma. We want to be around them, while we avoid those who are negative.

Now and then we've all experienced getting tired of someone, and dropping on the sofa when we get home, saying: "That person drains all my energy." NO! You are the one who thinks the thoughts, and you can thank yourself for losing your energy.

We grow weary when there is imbalance between the conscious and the subconscious. We weaken our system and lose physical vigor and strength. Sometimes I've caught myself thinking that my own thoughts tire me out, and that's exactly right.

*Of course all this begins when we are very young?*

Yes. We learned about colors when we were young, for example. We learned about pink, blue and all the other colors. When I was a young girl, white and black were colors, but now we know better because new knowledge has become available. Everything is developing, fortunately, and we also need to develop as humans.

*Many people today feel exhausted. We may believe that it's due to work or ordinary stress, but you believe that the reason is found at a deeper level?*

Yes, we also feel drained when others say things that we either consciously or subconsciously don't agree with.

*Now we've arrived at the other factor, the part of the iceberg that steers. Please explain more thoroughly what you mean by that.*

When we are in the womb of our mother and begin to move, Delta frequencies can be measured. From then on we register the feelings, thoughts and experiences of our mother and other impulses from her surroundings. We are not able to analyze until we are about seven years old. So the experiences that we've registered are stored as truths. We later build new truths that are based upon those stored truths. After the age of about seven, our ability to analyze becomes stronger and stronger, and we begin to form our own opinions. From about seven to twelve years of age we analyze and think more and more independently, expanding our truths based on new thoughts and experiences. During this time, we lay a strong foundation for our own independent truths, and they become a reality we relate to. When we learn something new later on, our left brain hemisphere will always compare the new information with the truths we've already stored.

This happens automatically and at a subconscious level. That's why it can be tiring for people when I come along with my analysis and my truths, because they have other truths stored in their subconscious. Even worse, this is how quarrels, arguments and even wars get started.

*When we talk about truths you often start talking about magnets. Please explain.*

I've been fascinated by magnets since I was very young, by the way the poles attract or push each other away. I used to play with them by putting one magnet under the surface of a table and another on top, and drew the one on top around by moving the one below.

After I started working with self-development, I found that the magnet is a good illustration of how we function as humans. The conscious part of us is the pole of the magnet that repels or sends out, and the subconscious part of us is the pole that attracts.

*You like metaphors? You talk about icebergs and magnets, and I know that you will come to mention hot air balloons!*

Ok, ok, I know that I use images when I speak, but it helps many people to "think in pictures." Besides, I think people get tired of hearing about hertz, brainwaves and facts—the things that you men are so fond of, said Deborah with a mischievous twinkle in her eye.

*Bull's eye. Continue.*

Thanks. The reason I think that magnets fit in here, is that when you move them towards each other, they suddenly smack together—and it's almost impossible to get them apart again.

That's what it's like for us too. I attract experiences according to the truths I have stored in my subconscious mind. We say, "I didn't want to attract that," but it happens again and again. Whether we want it or not, that is what we get.

When I talked about this at a course once, a participant said: "You've created a new law of nature!"

No, I haven't. It's been this way throughout the ages, but I want to focus on it now and show how we may change ourselves and the world.

*Doesn't this compare to when several people enter a room where there is a cat, and the cat automatically goes to the person who is allergic to the cat or very afraid of it? Because the person focuses on their fear or discomfort and thereby sends out strong signals?*

That's exactly right! I think most people have experienced this in some way, and this is about fear that is stored in the subconscious and therefore attracts. Just think of the times when you were in school, hadn't done your homework and sat there thinking "please, please don't call on me to answer!" Guess who got asked?

This is the most important message in this book: The fear, the phobias, and any conviction that you can't do anything successfully, can all be transformed so that you may break out of the vicious circle and create smooth flow. All that has been learned can be transformed.

You will find out how you can change what you have learned in the chapter about transformation. The brain is flexible (scientists call it plastic), and that means that you can create changes. It helps you to create new neural pathways, so that external changes can come about. If I hadn't created new neural pathways and transformed incidents in my own life, I wouldn't be alive today. No question about that.

*These are things that are not talked about enough?*

Mothers and fathers haven't learned enough about these things. We are told specifically what we should or should not eat or drink as well as what to do or not do while pregnant, but few talk about mental aspects.

*This is a fascinating theme, and I agree that the foundation for how one copes with challenges later in life is built in early years, perhaps even before we were born. I've thought about that a lot regarding my son, who we had longed for. We had tried for many years to have children, so when we finally succeeded, my wife decided to take it easy so nothing bad would happen. She may have overdone it, but the result was that our son is very calm. That is in fact one of the first things most people mention when they meet him for the first time. I'm not saying that he is never rowdy, but he has a remarkably calm and secure attitude about life.*

Yes, you know what? This is unbelievably important to learn about. My advice to pregnant women is to relax, stay calm, stay as positive about life as possible and think of the fantastic event that awaits them. I am convinced that this influences the little one.

*How do people react when you talk about this?*

When we first hear about this we often begin to feel guilt. Many questions come to mind. What did I think about when I was pregnant? What did I do? How has this affected my child? How has this affected my life?

I know that I have affected my children, but I also know that I, like most people, did the best I could based on what I knew at the time. The most difficult admission for me was that I, in fact, had influenced my children. I'm not saying this to give anyone a guilty conscience, but so that we can learn how we function as humans and influence others in a positive manner in the future.

When I was pregnant with my first child I was kicked in the abdomen by someone who was wearing safety boots, and I had to escape through a window. Just imagine what my feelings were like. I was afraid that my child would be injured and I was afraid that I would be injured. This is the kind of experience that a fetus can register when it is in its mother's womb. This kind of realization is painful of course, but at that point in my life I didn't know what I know today. If I'd been aware of how humans function, many incidents would have been avoided. This is why we must take these things seriously, and not just close our eyes to what we do not want to see.

*Is self-knowledge and some humorous distance to one's own life and methods something that is lacking in the "alternative world?"*

That may well be. I share many of my experiences when I teach a course, because this is natural for me. By sharing my own experiences and crises I show that what I am teaching is not just something that I am preaching, but are tools that I've had to use myself to cope with all of the challenges that have come my way. I continue to use these tools every single day.

Don't analyze *my* life. It's *your own* that you should analyze!

*I have the impression that many who begin self-development are looking for a crutch that can give them support in their lives. What do you say to them?*

I would say: "be your own crutch." There are no magic spells for a good life. It's even simpler in fact. You must understand your inner processes, learn how to change what you wish to change, find out why you want to make changes, set your focus, define goals, etc. None of this is mystical or supernatural, but it does require effort. Who wouldn't be willing to make an effort to change their lives for the better?

This manner of thinking changes the way you look upon the world. That is why it's natural to feel some resistance when you read this book.

I know that it sounds radical, but that's because we haven't learned enough about how we function as humans.

Why not give it a try? What do you have to lose by using a little time on something that can in fact transform your whole life?

*That's how I felt after having participated in a course. What can I lose? Reading the stories in this book about changes that others have brought about in their lives also makes one feel humble.*

Yes, and that is exactly why I continue to share so much from my own life, due to a genuine desire that the lives of others will also improve.

# Assignment for the second week

This week we will expand Exercise 1. The expansion involves adding a positive experience that you have had that makes you feel good. In this exercise you are to dream yourself into the exercise. By that I mean that you are to think about the sounds, fragrances, colors and feelings that you relate to the experience. If you, for example, are in a rose garden, think back to a time when you smelled a rose. This is training for your inner sense, to help create a magical daily life.

I recommend that you use this exercise at least once a day this week.

### Exercise 2: For expanded relaxation

- Start with Exercise 1: Counting down from 7 to 1. When you feel relaxed you may continue.
- Now choose a positive experience you have had and use a few minutes to dream that you are living the experience. Notice what you hear, the smells you recognize, the colors you see and the feelings you have during this experience.

When you want to conclude, use the procedure for counting out (see Exercise 1).

# *ESP: Your sixth sense*

ESP is an acronym for extra sensory perception. In other words, an extra sense we use to perceive non-physical information. Some call it a sixth sense. We use it when we get a creative idea. You don't use your five physical senses to perceive an idea. You can't see it with your eyes, hear it with your ears, smell it, physically taste it or physically touch the idea.

If you look at the iceberg, a creative idea comes from the subconscious. It often comes to us when our eyes are open. Our brain has then converted non-physical information perceived by our ESP sense. It may nonetheless feel like it is physical because we have our eyes open and because it is the physical world we are used to dealing with. Haven't you ever wondered where those good ideas come from?

Think of your brain as a converter. We have two languages, a physical and a non-physical. We perceive an idea using our ESP sense, and our brain converts or translates the idea to a physical language.

*How is this information received?*

We have three different ways to perceive non-physical information. One way is called kinesthetic, and this is information that comes through bodily sensations such as gut feelings.

Another way to perceive non-physical information is called auditory, and we get this information by hearing or thoughts, such as intuition.

The third way to perceive non-physical information is visual, through images in our mind's eye, as in our dreams.

One participant phoned me and told about a nightmare she had two nights in a row about a man who wanted to get into her house. Dreams are a visual way to perceive information. She was afraid, and at that time she was home alone. A few days later she felt as if the man appeared physically and wanted to tell her something while she was sitting and writing her Nightfilm. She tried to ask the man for an explanation, but received no answer. She became even more afraid. That's why she phoned me to ask about this, and it's a good example of how fear may grip you.

*You need to explain more.*

We have nightmares when we don't listen to what the subconscious tries to tell us. If we haven't learned to interpret our inner symbols, and therefore do not understand what it is that we are to perceive, our imagination can get out of control. Old fears may come up, such as fear of being alone or fear of the dark. For this person, her imagination created an illusion that she physically heard the man come. What the dream was communicating in this case, was that she needed to act physically to do something in her life.

*Can you give additional examples about perceiving non-physical information?*

Yes. At one course that I taught, I borrowed a wristwatch from a participant. As soon as it was in my hand I was filled with a feeling of sorrow. I asked in my mind what this was telling me, and I immediately felt freedom. I had to again ask myself what this was telling me. Then I got an idea: he lived in a street called "Sorrow-free Lane."

In this case I perceived sorrow and freedom kinesthetically, and auditory perception to hear an idea or just know.

A number of years ago I was being interviewed by a reporter in my home. I served coffee and we sat down by the kitchen table. I suddenly realized that my coffee smelled very strange, like newly poached codfish. I cautiously asked the reporter if her cup of coffee smelled like codfish, but she couldn't smell anything but coffee. Just then I received a text message on my cell phone from a friend who asked if I would like to come for dinner. Newly poached codfish was on the menu.

This example also shows a kinesthetic way to perceive non-physical information, through our sense of smell.

Another time I was to appear in court about a lawsuit. I had prepared a Nightfilm the evening before, and visualized myself with energy and enough strength to cope with the day. When I awoke that morning and was getting ready to leave, I started humming a tune that came into my head. It wouldn't go away. While riding in the car it persisted, and I couldn't remember what song it was. I asked a friend who was with me in the car if she could recognize that line of the tune that I was humming. She brought out her iPod and put the earphones up to my ears. I then heard the same tune, a song from the TV-series "Touched by an Angel." That was an answer to the Nightfilm about having enough strength to cope with my day in a good way. To me, an angel is a symbol of something good. In addition, this was an auditory way to perceive the answer, through hearing.

Another example was a time when a friend phoned me and said that his girlfriend was getting ready to travel, but her passport was missing. I saw an image in my mind's eye of a chest of drawers with the third drawer open. "Look in the chest of drawers in the hallway, it's in the third drawer," I said. They had already looked there, without finding it. "Look again," I said, "and call me when you've found it."

This was a visual way to perceive information. The fact that the third drawer was open told me where in the chest of drawers it was. Knowing that the chest of drawers was in the hallway was auditory information.

The story ended with another phone call; the passport had been found in the third drawer of the chest of drawers in the hallway.

When I worked as a business manager, we were once sitting in a meeting about a contract. During the meeting I had a strong feeling that something was wrong, and I asked for a break. My boss wondered about the interruption, and I had to explain that my gut feeling told me that something was not right. He relied on that, and we didn't sign the contract. A week later we found out that the company we had been negotiating with was bankrupt.

Many people remember similar experiences, but often do not rely on the signals they get. This was, again, a kinesthetic way of perceiving information—through a gut feeling.

Becoming familiar with yourself and how you perceive your information is important for the way your life flows. You need to know how you function in order to get correct information for a magical daily life.

We use all three ways of perceiving non-physical information, but one of them is often dominant.

*Are you saying that this was what you used in "Sensing Murder?"*

Yes, and that's one of the reasons that I agreed to participate. My goal was to show that we all have an ESP sense—or gut feelings, as we often call it. As a business leader, it's great to use gut feelings, and many are praised for that. However, when I say that I use my gut feelings, some people look strangely at me. Interesting, for it's the same gut feeling—but I use mine consciously and for many other purposes.

A lot of people think that the ESP sense means seeing images. Images in our mind can be quite tiring, and they must be interpreted, since they symbolize something. An example of this is the forest where I was searching for the place where a murder victim was found. How could I have found the right place if I had only had an image in my mind? Only trees and more trees were in that forest.

By understanding how I perceive non-physical information and put it all together, the information becomes correct and useful.

We all experience things differently, depending on what we've experienced. In addition, our brain brings forth the last familiar experience.

While searching in that forest I also had to make choices. Should I go this way or that way? In situations like that it's important to make a choice and go for it. If you start analyzing too much you will suddenly have several alternatives and the choice becomes difficult. Uncertainty enters the picture, and we become incapable of action.

---

On Monday, August 30, 1999 the following article appeared in *Drammens Tidende*, a local newspaper:

### Man missing in Hemsedal Valley

A man in his late thirties was reported missing in Hemsedal Valley on Saturday evening. The man, originally from Oslo, was living in the family's cabin. The family reported him missing at 6:30 PM Saturday evening after having searched for him for a long while. About 30 persons from Red Cross started a search that lasted until midnight Saturday and was resumed at 9:00 AM on Sunday. "On Monday morning we will consider resuming the search again," said Anne-Kari Eriksen from the police. The search was stopped at 9:00 PM Sunday. Eriksen described the terrain as steep hills that are difficult to search.

---

*This case was peculiar, Deborah, even for you with all your experience.*

Yes, you can say that. I think it's a good example of how ESP can work in different ways and with a comprehensive perspective.

Three years after the man was reported missing, I was contacted by his cousin who had seen me in the media. At the time I was working with the filming of "Sensing Murder."

I told him that I don't work with cases like that, since they are the responsibility of the police and ordinary citizens shouldn't interfere. There was nonetheless something that made me feel I should help in this case.

*How did the process start?*

I was given the name of the missing person and was shown a photo of him and a wallet with a bank card. I immediately saw an image in my mind's eye of mountainous landscape that I described in detail, with a farm where he'd been living in a cabin, etc.

I also saw where he had walked, and right away got a feeling that he was no longer alive.

*How did you know that?*

I felt cold, and for me that is kinesthetic information that something is dead. The cousin nonetheless asked if I would come to the mountain valley to look for the dead body, so the family could experience closure and have a grave to go to.

I was very much in doubt, but finally agreed and went to Hemsedal Valley and met the people who lived on the farm where the missing man had lived.

When I arrived, I saw that the place looked just as I had imagined, so I decided to follow the same route I had perceived that the missing man had followed.

The body wasn't far away from the farm. In a way I knew where it was, but didn't feel I should go there with the family. I had a very strong feeling that it would be traumatic for them to find the remains of their close relative.

I thought that I needed to find some other solution for this dilemma. Suddenly I found myself saying to them: "We're stopping now. In a week's time you will receive a message from the police that someone has found remains of the body. The police will tell you that they found a boot with a foot in it."

*Good grief! Where did you get that idea?*

I don't know, I just said it, and it felt right to stop right then and there.

It's not healthy for family members to be there for experiences like that. When we use our ESP sense in a good way, it will not always be exactly as we expected, or as the skeptics expect, but will be best for everyone, for the whole.

*What happened then?*

That was on a Sunday. On the following Saturday someone from the farm phoned me and said: "Deborah, the police just called and said that a hiker has found a boot with the remains of a foot in it."

He continued by saying that the police had become very interested, for as soon as the officer had presented himself, the man had answered: "Oh, have you found a boot with remains of a foot in it?"

It became quite silent, then the officer asked in amazement where the man had heard that.

This seems to me to be the best ending for this case. The relatives received their answers, while the actual discovery was made by a hiker who was not personally involved in the case.

*How did you concretely proceed in order to get this information, if I may ask?*

I used a Nightfilm to envision myself solving the case, as described in the chapter about the Nightfilm technique in this book.

---

On August 29, 2002 the following appeared in *Hallingdølen*, another local newspaper:

**May solve mysterious disappearance**

A hiker in Hemsedal Valley recently found something that may solve a three-year old disappearance.

On Saturday, August 28, 1999 a man in his late 30's was reported missing. The discovery by the hiker is being considered in relation to that disappearance. The hiker found material that indicates that the man disappeared in a precise area in Hemsedal Valley, not far from the place where the man had been living before he disappeared.

**Waiting for answer**

According to information received by *Hallingdølen*, this is about signs that may give answers about the mysterious disappearance. Some material has been sent to the Institute for Forensic Medicine for DNA analysis. The Police have not yet received the analysis, and therefore do not want to say exactly where the material was found. "The reason is that we have planned an extensive search with specially trained dogs in the area this week," said Bent Øye, a representative for the local police.

# Imagination: Friend or foe?

"Imagination is more important than knowledge. Knowledge is limited. Imagination encircles the world."
—Albert Einstein (1879–1955)

*You talk a lot about imagination and how it affects all that we do. How does that work?*

The left brain hemisphere examines details and doesn't see anything else. We can therefore get stuck in old incidents it has fetched from the archive. It works systematically, and that's an important quality. It helps us retain balance. The right brain hemisphere works without analyzing and floats around. Imagination is also in the right hemisphere, and if given free reign, imagination can complicate the situation and create a lot of strange things.

While daydreaming, some fear may arise from the subconscious and become our worst enemy. It's important to strengthen the ESP sense to understand what we receive, so we don't let our imagination run wild.

*So "good imagination," that we often mean as a compliment, isn't always positive?*

No, but imagination can also be your best friend. In that case we use our imagination to create positive events. Today my imagination has become my best friend, and helps me to create a good life, a magical daily life.

It hasn't always been that way. Earlier in my life my imagination was often my worst enemy. I had a vivid imagination; fears came over me and I ran away from life without knowing it. I created a lot of anxiety, not because I wanted to, but because I didn't understand. There was a time when I didn't dare go to my mailbox or to the store.

*That doesn't sound good at all.*

You bet. I had to get my children to go in and do the shopping, while I sat in the car. My imagination was allowed to take over, and I was filled with anxiety. An example that many recognize in themselves, is when someone we agreed to meet is late and we stand there waiting. The first ten minutes are OK, but as time passes we begin to look at the clock more and more often. Suddenly thoughts arise about what could have gone wrong. Finally, if enough time passes, we may find ourselves imagining a funeral. When we haven't learned to take control of our imagination, we allow it to churn and churn. Thoughts influence our body, we become tense and experience more and more pain in our body. We inflict pain upon ourselves through thoughts, because the brain doesn't know the difference between a thought and an action, and chemical reactions are triggered.

Let's do a little experiment with our thoughts. Imagine that you are really living this experiment. Read slowly while you think that you are doing what I say.

Think that I'm standing in front of you with a large yellow lemon. I invite you into the kitchen. We're standing by a cutting board, and I take a knife and cut the lemon in two. Now you can see that lemon juice drips out of the lemon and makes a little puddle on the cutting board. I show you the juicy insides of the lemon. Now I cut one of the halves in two, and more lemon juice runs out. Then I ask you to pick up one of the pieces of lemon and take a bite. Put it in your mouth and take a good bite.

Did you have any physical reactions to this thought experiment? Perhaps saliva in your mouth, wrinkling your nose or tasting something sour in your mouth? Perhaps your jaws tightened? Whatever you experienced, it shows that thoughts influence the body; the brain gives signals as if you in fact did this experiment physically, and not just read about it.

That is how we create with our thoughts.

*It sounds like you have a lot of experience with fear. What were, or are, you afraid of?*

I've had a lot of fear in my life. I was afraid of the dark, of being alone, of heights, elevators—most everything. What happens? Let's consider my fear of elevators. My mother also feared them, and I was often with my mother when I was young. I learned to beware the elevator, because it could get stuck. We climbed 12 flights of stairs rather than take the elevator. We learn quickly when we are young, and I was a fast learner. Things become automatic and rapidly become habits. I also had a vivid imagination, and when I was older I saw movies where people got stuck in elevators that were dark, where gases seeped in and they were slowly suffocated. I felt it was real, and had breathing problems every time I approached an elevator.

Another example was that I learned to be afraid of wasps. I learned that very early as well; we were to stand up, scream and wave our arms until the wasp was gone. It feels foolish to act like that at a garden party where the table is nicely decorated, red wine is on the table, and women are wearing nice dresses. It may lead to an embarrassing situation, and what was learned does not serve us well any longer. Due to that fear I also developed an allergy to wasp bites, and I taught my children the same—that was the way to react to wasps. Not because I was mean, but because I thought that was the way it was supposed to be. That kind of learning is inherited.

We also learn at an early age that we cannot do things. Children learn very quickly that they cannot do something, without even trying. I believe that they learn that they cannot. Parents are quick to do things for children. Stand here, let mother do it. Just wait there, dad will fix that. As adults we are then saying to the subconscious mind of children that you cannot do it, so we do it for you.

This quickly becomes a thought that the child adopts. When this automatizes, what happens when they become adults? We can't do that, and if we try to do something that we cannot do, then performance anxiety kicks in, then self-criticism, and we are then in a negative spiral. This leads to great limitation in life, and it's important to remember that the mechanisms that create positive flow work in the same way when they are used negatively. Then "everything goes wrong" and the flow is negative.

Now I've been able to change that attitude. I do as I like, even when I haven't done it before. That also gives me a more exciting and interesting life.

*I remember when I became a father. After five minutes the midwife placed the infant in my arms and said: "Let's go and bathe the baby." I was panic stricken and stuttered that I couldn't do that. She calmed me down and helped me, and I believe that incident helped me to gain a very natural attitude towards caring for babies—something I didn't think I could do.*

That is what is most fascinating about self-development, and it becomes even more exciting when we discover that what we have learned can be unlearned, or we can create and learn something new. The brain creates a new neural pathway, and when it has done that enough times it becomes automatic, or a truth for us.

If we let our imagination run wild, without control, we create an awful life for ourselves. The way we react in various situations is based on what is stored in our subconscious mind.

We are taught to place limits on ourselves, to behave politely and pleasantly. What happens then? Things pile up inside of us and we explode when we least expect it. For example, an unpleasant atmosphere can develop at the table because one of the children has been unfortunate and spilled a glass of milk. This is sad for the child, who was only unlucky while still in training.

I often say that people walk around like ticking bombs because we don't process our feelings. I walked around like that, carrying many unprocessed feelings that resulted in ill health in my case. In extreme cases it can lead to violence resulting in death.

*Now we're at the core of what you are working for?*

Yes, my great dream is that we get a subject in schools that teaches us about how we function as humans, and how we can cope with unprocessed feelings. I consider this book to be a step in that direction. Someone must dare to share, so that we can become conscious humans who act in a reflective manner and thereby avoid emotional outbursts that hurt others.

We must learn to take control of our imagination and thoughts in order to live a good life. You can choose your thoughts. In addition, you must remember the three different ways of receiving non-physical information, as explained in the chapter on *ESP: Your sixth sense.* The visual way of receiving leads to many misunderstandings, since imagination can make the images seem to be alive when the brain projects things out into the physical. If we see an angel or a monster, we can use our imagination to make them seem to be alive.

Think about dreams, they can be experienced as quite real. The ESP sense continually fetches information from all directions. Time and space do not exist where that sense functions. If you receive information in an auditory way, you might in fact "hear visions." One example is a type of premonition that Norwegians refer to. I can remember an episode a few years ago when my daughter was home alone while I was teaching a course. I was looking forward to seeing her again and thought a lot about her on my way home. Her auditory ESP sense perceived my thoughts, and when I came home she told me that she heard me arrive five minutes before I actually did. That is how our ESP sense can function when we receive information through intuition.

The left brain hemisphere always tries to understand by using earlier experiences. It then finds something that has been seen, heard or felt earlier and processes that. This means that humans do not get the same signals when we seek to understand something. It will be interpreted based on what each individual learned earlier. Your consciousness while awake is limited to what you have already experienced. It is therefore important for me to pass on the insight I have about how our mind functions, so that we all can expand our consciousness.

The left brain hemisphere is controlled by the will, while the right brain hemisphere is controlled by feelings and imagination. The imagination always wins. As with the magnet, both brain hemispheres must draw in the same direction in order to get what you want.

# The Creative Corner

*What exactly is "The Creative Corner?"*

When I created the course, I got an idea to call my inner room "The Creative Corner." In addition to being a definite place inside myself, it describes a state of creativity and genius. Many have heard the expression: "being in the creative corner."

*Is that what the bible refers to as "go into your room?"*

You're on to something there. It's interesting to see how elements of meditation, relaxation and reflection are found in almost all religions and cultures. As you know, I like to be more down-to-earth.

Think that you build an inner room and decide that it is your creative haven. There you can create new things and transform the old. You may build it exactly as it suits you. A room you can furnish as you like. You may build additional rooms if you like. If you don't want a room, you may choose to create a place. It can be anything you decide.

*Is it OK for me to choose a place that I know well, where I feel comfortable?*

No, it's not that simple. You must use your imagination to create something that is only for you and that does not exist physically. You may for example choose a cabin, but not one that you know. You must build your own. This is also a way to improve creativity, in addition to creating new, positive experiences.

This inner room is to be associated with inner tranquility, creativity and balance.

My inner room is by the sea, where I can be outside and enjoy the stillness and sounds from the sea. I also have a house there, furnished in a way that is useful for me. This place has developed through the years, just as I've been developing. The Creative Corner mirrors ourselves. We will talk more about The Creative Corner in later chapters.

*I'm less imaginative. My room is just a room without any decorations, just two comfortable arm chairs.*

That doesn't matter, as long as it works for you. You are a little macho, so interior design is perhaps not important for you, said Deborah with a smile.

# Assignment for the third week

This week we will expand the exercise by creating your own inner room. This room will then be The Creative Corner, the starting point for your inner work.

I recommend using The Creative Corner at least once a day this week. You may use it to relax with good experiences and/or create or further change the room.

### Exercise 3: Extended relaxation in The Creative Corner
- You start with exercises 1 and 2, and when you have thought about your positive experience for a while, you are ready to proceed.
- Focus your attention on your chest. Think that you enter a room within yourself. Use plenty of time to create an inner room.

When you have created your inner room and want to conclude the session, use the procedure for counting out (see Exercise 1).

# Affirmations: A simple tool for creating magical days

"Every day and in every way I become better and better."
—Emile Coué (1857–1926)

*I've noticed that people who don't know each other well, often start talking about something terrible that's happened. Almost immediately someone says "yes, that's awful!" and that starts a conversation. It is true that there are a lot of terrible things happening in the world, but there's a lot of good and positive too. Perhaps focus should be on that the next time?*

Before I started my self-development, I had periods where I felt that life got worse and worse—more and more unbearable. Today I often overhear someone say "Yes, that's the way it's supposed to be. It will never get better." or something like that.

In the chapter about truths we talked about how we store experiences and incidents and take them with us throughout life. From the age of six or seven, analysis becomes possible. That is, we start analyzing and questioning things. Not all of our thoughts are necessarily helpful. When we think the same thought over and over again, it becomes a truth in our lives. If we have many negative thoughts, our lives are greatly influenced by that.

*Considering everything you've carried with you from younger years, you've probably used a lot of time on this?*

You bet! I've worked a lot with replacing thoughts that didn't help me to progress. I had, for example, sneaking thoughts that I couldn't do anything, that I wasn't good enough, etc. Affirmations have helped me become conscious of the thoughts I want to have and the ones I don't want.

*Give us some examples of sentences that you use.*

They can apply for everyone. We are not so different after all, at least when it comes to problems and complexes.

One of them is: "I am willing to create changes in myself."

This is a sentence that helps us to open up for change, which can be frightening. One might also think that if change is necessary, then we are not good enough as we are. Of course we are, and change in that event will just make life even better.

The next sentence is for me quite self-evident, but perhaps not for everyone? "Positive thoughts and positive attitudes help me to a better life."

Another sentence is: "I am worthy, and I enjoy every moment."

Feeling that one is worthy is basic for seeing the good in life and enjoying every moment, but feeling worthy is not necessarily present in us.

Another example is: "I am patient with myself and others."

Most people are too self-critical. We are not very patient with ourselves. In addition, we've learned at an early age that if others don't understand the same as I do, they are dumb. That is of course not the case, and we need to respect each other for who we are, and be patient.

*I have for many years led creative processes in ad agencies, regarding TV-programs and the like. All of these processes begin with an idea phase where the goal is to come up with as many ideas as possible and thereafter sort and evaluate them. During the first phase it's very important to encourage as many ideas as possible, so then we must say "yes, and" instead of "yes, but" every time someone contributes a suggestion. This is very difficult for many. Research exists that confirms that the natural reaction to all new ideas is skepticism. I usually say, "relax, in an hour we'll evaluate each suggestion critically," and then most people calm down.*

Yes, I recognize that pattern from my courses. There's always someone who resists, because they intuitively understand that they are doing something that can change their lives, and that is something that many fear, even when they are not well off where they are. That sounds strange, but that's how it is. It's a type of defense mechanism.

But Kim, you have a story about how affirmations can create smoother flow in life and bring about quite extensive positive changes?

*Yes, I do, and I hope it can get more people to come to grips with difficult situations and discover that it is in fact considerably easier to climb out of the quagmire than one often thinks.*

*A while back I experienced problems at work. The company I worked for had been sold to a foreign company and was moving in the wrong direction, as I saw it. In addition I realized that my position might become unnecessary in the new organization.*

*I understood that I needed to find another job as quickly as possible. The problem was that I worked in a small field of business that had been hit by the financial crisis at that time. I was in addition in my late fifties, and as such was not particularly attractive in a field that cultivates youth—or in any field for that matter. The odds for finding a good job, or any job at all, were not very good. What should I do?*

*I found myself in a crisis, something we all experience in life from time to time. What many people do—and what I also did earlier—was to think about everything negative that this situation brought with it, until we finally sit in a quagmire of negativity. This makes us even more downcast and unable to act. For some this situation becomes so unbearable that their marriage breaks up. Some choose intoxication to drown the depression, and for some life becomes so hopeless that they choose suicide.*

What you are describing now, Kim, is what we may call negative flow. We find ourselves in a kind of negative quagmire that is more and more difficult to get out of.

*Yes, but through your course I learned how to cope with such situations. It's just as easy to create positive flow as negative flow, if one just wants to and believes it strongly enough—and knows how to get started.*

*I did this: I thought about all the times I had experienced crisis. When looking back, what I saw was that something good had come out of all of those crises. I had learned something, and life became better. I therefore sat down and said to myself: "Something positive comes from this!"*

*Every time I began to think negative thoughts, I said to myself: "Stop thinking like that, you know that this results in something positive!" I don't know how many times a day I said that to myself—but it was many!*

What happened?

*I had set a goal for myself that this situation would end up being positive. I knew that I had to take charge and do something myself. Of course, nothing positive comes by itself if you just sit on your butt and repeat that it will happen. However, convincing myself that this would end up positive resulted in more energy and drive for me to do what was necessary.*

*I called the person responsible for the largest TV-company in Norway and asked if they had a job for me. I did this even though I "knew" that they did not. "If we don't have one, we'll make one," was his answer. We signed a contract a week later, and I had a new job. I landed a lucrative agreement with my previous employer and received a generous bonus for terminating. I left my previous job without bad feelings for me or my previous colleagues.*

*Now I've been in the new job for half a year. It's more fun than any job I've ever had. I'm surrounded by a group of people who have the same attitude as I do about how a production company could be run. I look forward to going to work every day.*

*"You were so lucky," some say. "You just made a phone call and everything fell into place." "Not at all," I said. "I created my own good luck." That is what smooth flow is about. When you are in the smooth flow zone, you pay more attention to your gut feelings and make the right decisions.*

*I realize that much of this can sound like a cliché. "Something positive can come out of this," and hocus pocus, everything gets solved? It's just that it really works! I understand that it can be hard to accept. I myself was more than skeptical the first time I heard about it. Now I don't bother wasting time wondering why or how. I know that it works, and that's enough for me.*

That's great, Kim, that's exactly the conclusion I came to as well. I developed techniques that helped create smooth flow, and I no longer wasted time by being skeptical. My philosophy is simple. Use what works, and don't remain sitting where things have come to a halt. Many have said to me that what I'm doing isn't for them, and every time I wonder what they mean, when I see them bathing in their negative quagmire. You've surely heard the expression from Einstein: "Insanity is doing the same things again and again, and expecting a new result." I therefore don't understand people who prefer to remain sitting in the mud, when there is another way.

Using oneself in a new way can give results at every level in life.

Affirmations are a part of becoming more aware, but if you want lasting change you need to transform in The Creative Corner. I remember when I started my process of self-development and I posted affirmations all around the house, visible to all. I wrote on slips of paper, and affirmations were everywhere, even in the bathroom. It's really a good illustration: out with the old and in with something new.

I remember the very first sentence the kinesiologist gave me to repeat: "I accept myself." Every time I said that, my inner voice answered: "no you don't" or "now you're lying." I had to repeat that sentence until the inner voice gave up.

A French psychologist and pharmacologist, Emile Coué (1857–1926), taught his patients to say the sentence: "Every day and in every way, I become better and better." This was so effective that he stopped using hypnosis and started using affirmations for his patients.

A course participant used "I have smooth flow" as a computer password. I feel that's a good example of how one can integrate positive thinking in daily life.

# Assignment for the fourth week

This week we will add affirmations to exercises 1, 2 and 3.

When you work with affirmations, repeat each affirmation to yourself ten times, one at a time. It's important to understand what the sentence means and feel yourself living it. It will then quickly become a truth for you.

I recommend using this exercise at least once a day.

Learn the affirmations by heart before doing the exercise.

### Exercise 4: For expanded relaxation with affirmations

- Start by doing exercises 1, 2 and 3. When you are in The Creative Corner and have calmed down, you may continue.
- Say the following four affirmations to yourself and repeat each one ten times:
    - I am willing to create changes in myself.
    - Positive thoughts and positive attitudes help me to a better life.
    - I am worthy, and I enjoy every moment.
    - I am patient with myself and others.

When you are finished with the affirmations and want to conclude the session, use the procedure for counting out described in Exercise 1.

# Summary of basic exercise for relaxation

In the course of four weeks you have worked your way through the four exercises that are the foundation for the basic exercise for relaxation. In the first exercise you established a basis for physical relaxation. Exercise two laid the foundation for inner tranquility and harmony. In the third exercise you established a foundation for balance between the outer physical and the creative inner, and The Creative Corner was established. The fourth exercise helped you to hold focus, so that you may succeed in the work ahead.

The whole basic exercise is summarized here. I recommend doing this exercise once each day. The exercise will help you to better health, inner calmness and more stamina. This is a healthy alternative to a nap. If you want music in the background, I feel that peaceful instrumentals are a good choice.

### Basic exercise

- Sit down and find a comfortable position with your hands resting in your lap. Close your eyes.
- Take a deep breath, and while exhaling think of the number 7 and focus your attention on your scalp.
- Let go of all stress and all worries, and feel your scalp relaxing. Give yourself plenty of time.
- Think that there is a light right above your head. You decide what this light is like. The light is to help you to relax.
- Then think that you allow the light to flow downward and spread out, covering your entire scalp.
- When your scalp feels relaxed, proceed to the number 6 and repeat as above, but with focus on your forehead. Then you continue working downward until you reach number 1.
- Number 6 is your forehead.
- Number 5 is your throat. In addition, let the light spread around your neck and down to cover your shoulders, arms and hands, as well as down your back.

- Number 4 is your chest.
- Number 3 is your stomach area, between your lower ribs.
- Number 2 is your abdomen.
- Number 1 is the bottom of your torso.
- When you are finished with number 1, allow the light to flow down both of your legs simultaneously: down your thighs, knees, calves and out in both feet.
- Now choose a positive experience for you, and use a few minutes to dream as if you are in this experience. Pay attention to what you may hear, fragrances you may smell, colors you may see and feelings you have during this experience.
- Take a deep breath and think that you go into The Creative Corner.
- Say the following affirmations to yourself:
  o I am willing to create changes in myself.
  o Positive thoughts and positive attitudes help me to a better life.
  o I am worthy, and I enjoy every moment.
  o I am patient with myself and others.

## Counting out

- First, decide to end this exercise.
- Think of the number 1, then begin to carefully move your toes, then your lower legs, followed by moving your entire legs. Use a few seconds to do this.
- Think of the number 2 and begin to move your fingers, your hands and then your entire arms, while you prepare to awaken.
- Think of the number 3. Open your eyes and say to yourself: I am now wide awake and feel as if I've had a good night's sleep.

# The Nightfilm technique:
## Getting rid of worries and taking control in your own life

"When one door closes another one opens, but we so often look so long and so regretfully upon the closed door, that we don't see the ones which open for us"

—Alexander Graham Bell
(1847–1922)

*In the course, you teach participants a tool that you call the Nightfilm technique. What it's about is that just before going to sleep, you are to let go of your worries by writing them down—and then describe important events that you want to happen the next day. In the stories that some participants have contributed in this book, a number of examples are given of how this has been used. Later we'll describe the technique in detail, but can you first tell us about the background?*

Our left brain hemisphere represents our intellect, while our right brain hemisphere represents our intelligence. Together they give us enormous potential.

As I said earlier, Arthur Schopenhauer described intelligence as the innate possibilities that humans are born with, and our intelligence never sleeps.

Jill Bolte Taylor describes how the right brain hemisphere perceives things as fluid. Think of a TV-picture that is disturbed so that we perceive it as pixels. There is no stable form, as it is the left brain hemisphere that creates the stable (physical) form.

Sometimes we experience something around us that we cannot see, a type of information that we don't have any experience with, something that the left brain hemisphere cannot put into perspective. It will then retrieve earlier experiences and try to understand the information by using our five physical senses and the three ways to perceive ESP information: kinesthetic, auditory and visual. We talked about this in the chapter about the ESP sense.

It's in our creative inner level that we can experience greater wholeness. I have used this creative inner level and learned to understand it, and I've experienced how important it is for balancing our lives.

*It's here that Delta brainwave frequencies come in?*

Yes, when we gain access to our possibilities in this way, we use the deepest level of sleep, Delta, together with the highest frequencies, Gamma, and attain an alert state with empathy, without the dominating human ego. There is a feeling of enormous love that can move one to tears. I can understand that this contact with ourselves makes us want more of it, and only that. The more we try, however, the stronger our ego becomes, and we move away from that level and up to the Theta, Alpha and Beta brainwave frequency levels.

At this deep Delta level—scientists call this state "connectedness"— we gain access to smooth flow and reach the essence of ourselves. You may have noticed that you and others might say: "I'm not really like that," or "That's not how I really want to be." We know at some level in ourselves what we are. We *are* in fact lucky and fortunate. It's natural for us to create smooth flow and live a happy life. We've just forgotten how.

I know that you have examples of smooth flow that influence your days, Kim.

*Yes, I use gut feelings to get smooth flow every day, and in very ordinary situations. For example: we live in a house with an old oil furnace. During the winter it broke down, and winter 2010 was cold! It was imperative to get it repaired or replaced. I had to contact a plumber immediately, and we needed one who could come the same day. I used Google to make a list of plumbers and started dialing the number to the first company. When I had hit the first four digits I suddenly thought: "No, not them—use the one that is third on the list. I stopped dialing the first number and dialed the third one instead. A very friendly plumber said that I was really lucky, since one of their larger jobs had been postponed an hour ago, so they could send someone right away.*

You were really lucky, Deborah laughed.

*He-he, I considered telling the plumber about using gut feelings, but decided to wait until he was finished with the job.*

*I know that living according to these principles sounds strange, but when we've accepted that it works, we stop thinking about that. I've philosophized about why people are so skeptical to using such techniques in their lives. One of the strangest things is that many of those who are most skeptical have no problem accepting that this is a common method for top-level athletics.*

*A good example is one of our fantastic cross-country skiers who, after having won a race by 10 cm, was asked how he had managed to mobilize his reserves and cross the finish line first. "I closed my eyes and saw myself on top of the winners' rostrum." Or the soccer player that curled an impossible free kick into the top corner, leaving the keeper with no chance to block it: "While I was approaching the ball, I saw the ball score a goal." We've read and heard this type of interview ever so often, and accept these statements without batting an eye. Why then is it so difficult to use the same techniques in our own lives? "All good athletes must have a good portion of luck," it's said. No! All good athletes must have a good portion of smooth flow! Smooth flow is about being in balance and following one's own gut feeling, or call it instinct if you feel that gut feeling sounds too frightening.*

*You say that we, to begin with, must consider ourselves to be connected with all others, as a community. You need to explain this, Deborah.*

Again I will use one of my metaphors: Think of a computer. What you put in, is what you get out. You write a document and can print it out by using a printer. If you want to change something, you must open the document to make the changes before you can print the corrected version. All of this may be stored on the hard disk drive. When connected to a network, all information from all of the computers in the network may be stored on a server.

If we now transfer this image to us humans, we can say that we all have a computer and it is portable, we are small laptops. We store new documents and we update stored documents. We can delete and we can change. When we are at the deepest sleep level, Delta, we are connected to the server—there where you and I share a common existence, or connectedness. The server is updated with your information and mine. All information is stored on the server, so I can be updated with your information and you with mine. There is always information available from everyone, in a universal community.

*No wonder so many crazy things happen—there's always so much trouble with computer networks!*

Stop fooling around now, this is important! Deborah looks sternly over her reading glasses.

The ESP sense helps us to get information during the course of the day. That's why it's important that it is well trained, and that we understand the information we get. We must, in addition, have access to the network, and we get that when we're in a calm state with low brainwave frequencies.

In short, the Nightfilm helps us to let go of worries, get a good night's sleep and become updated with good solutions and new possibilities the following day.

We've all heard people who've said that they're going to "sleep on it," or "ponder about it for a few days" before making a decision. This is an important element of the Nightfilm.

*What is it that in fact happens when we "sleep on it?"*

Think about times when we need to make a choice or a decision. We think about it during the day, and we think about it before going to sleep. Our brainwave frequencies are then slowing down to a lower tempo—Alpha frequencies—which is quite natural when we're tired. Sometimes we lie there thinking for a long time before we finally fall asleep. While asleep we also reach the deepest sleep level, Delta frequencies, and we're then connected to the network and the server, where solutions for the whole are found. We are updated with information. When we wake up—sometimes in the middle of the night—we know what to do. At other times we're "coincidentally" led to solutions, or we "coincidentally" meet the right people who can help, or smooth flow leads us to solutions that we could not have thought of ourselves.

*When we talk to others about such experiences, we often hear comments such as "Now you were really lucky," "How fortunate you are," or "Some people have it all."*

Yes, isn't that so! But we are *all* born lucky—born with good fortune. We can all create good solutions and a good life. When we begin moving as a fetus in our mother's womb, Delta frequencies can be measured, as we saw on the illustration earlier in this book, and we retain that frequency during our first year of life. As I see it, this is a natural state for us, before all the limitations and learning come about and we develop higher and higher frequencies. We also begin to analyze at about six or seven years of age, and we lose sight of the possibilities we were born with.

*Is that why most everyone instinctively reacts positively towards babies?*

Yes, they radiate Delta, and we think of them as wonderful, lovely and beautiful. Honestly, they are not all that beautiful—they are quite wrinkled in the beginning—but we don't see that. They are in Delta and radiate love and happiness, and they help us to feel the same.

This state of Delta and smooth flow is quite magical, a touching feeling of never-ending goodness where everything just falls into place. It's about being alive NOW, being present in life. I was everywhere else. I was stuck in the past and also thought about what the future would bring. My life wasn't magical, but filled with worries.

*Is that when you began to read Dale Carnegie?*

Yes, that book gave me some tips about how I could prepare for the following day, and that leads me to another important element in the Nightfilm technique: getting rid of concerns and worries by writing them down before preparing for the following day. As I said, we go around with loads of worries about the past and the future, so much that we're not able to be present in our own lives. We stand there hammering on closed doors and don't see opportunities that are right in front of us. With help from the Nightfilm technique, you connect yourself to a network of possibilities.

Getting rid of concerns and worries by writing them down has been good therapy for me. You put them down on paper, and then they don't bother you as much. Another thing is that what we focus upon has a tendency to grow, and I didn't want my concerns and worries to grow. By writing them down I could let go of them and focus instead on how I wanted the next day to be. The server was updated at the same time, and I opened myself for receiving something new.

*I remember that you mentioned something about the fight or flight mechanism and the force in us that mobilizes. Can you tell us more about that?*

Yes, that's a good description of what we experience at the Delta brainwave level when in danger or in difficult situations. We experience that we have access to unimaginable strength. One example is a mother who manages to lift a car to save her child who lies under it. We often say: "I don't know how I got the strength to get through that tough time."

I've experienced something like that myself. Once I had been given a lift home from work and was on my way into the apartment building where I lived in Oslo. A gang was sitting there on the lawn, and suddenly one of them came up to me and grabbed me, putting a knife to my throat. I became unbelievably calm while they discussed whether they should kill me or let me go. I was allowed to go, and my reaction came when I was safely inside the apartment building. My whole body trembled.

Another example happened just a few years ago. I had picked up my daughter after surgery. She was sitting in the back of the car resting, while I was driving southwards from Oslo in Friday rush-hour traffic on the highway. While approaching a tunnel, I suddenly had a feeling that I needed to pay attention to the car ahead of me. There were two lanes, and my car was in the left lane. The car in front of me veered over to the right lane, then back again. I said "hold on" to my daughter and then the rest happened as if in slow motion. The car ahead veered over again and hit the car in the right lane. It looked like it was being thrown back towards us. I saw pieces of metal and glass everywhere. Suddenly we came out of the tunnel and I stopped down the road, with both of us quite shaky. It wasn't until we arrived home and my daughter was safely in bed that I had a reaction. The accident replayed in my head several times and my whole body trembled. Fortunately no one was injured in the accident. The only damage was to the cars, but there wasn't a scratch on my car.

It's important to me that everyone knows that we all can gain access to this force within ourselves in our daily lives, not just when we're in danger or go through difficult periods in life. Then we can experience the state of smooth flow more often, an amazing and wonderful way of life.

# Assignment for the fifth week

This week you are to do the basic exercise for relaxation in addition to using the Nightfilm technique. I recommend that you do the relaxation exercise at least once a day, and write a Nightfilm every evening.

Research shows that using a pen and paper gives better results than writing on a computer, so I recommend that you use a notebook for your Nightfilms. You write in this notebook every evening in order to achieve lasting changes in your life. You don't need to think about nice handwriting or how much you write, but the writing itself is important. Do it just before going to bed or sitting up in bed when you're ready to retire for the night.

Read through the description of the technique and the examples before you start.

### Exercise 5: The Nightfilm technique

- Write "The Day Today" at the top of the page. On this page you are to write about how your day has been, including any challenges you may have encountered. Write about all of your emotions so that you let go of worried thoughts.
- When you've done that, write "The Day Tomorrow" as a heading. Under this heading you're to write about how you would like your day to be tomorrow. Write as if it has already happened. Conclude by writing: "Many thanks for a fantastic day with smooth flow and solutions for the whole." This sentence, or a similar expression of thanks, creates an expectation of smooth and positive flow in your daily life.
- When the written part is finished, it's time to do the mental stage where you connect yourself to the "server" to update and get updated, so that coincidences, good solutions and smooth flow come to you. The mental stage should be done sitting, to avoid falling asleep.

- Sit in your bed when you're ready to go to sleep. Close your eyes, take a deep breath and count from 7 to 1, taking a deep breath before each number. When you've reached number 1, assume that you are in your inner room.
- Think again through the day you had today, as if you're observing a movie. When you think of the day you've had in this way, you see everything that has happened from a distance and you don't relive the emotions.
- Think again through your day tomorrow, this time as if you are participating in the movie. Experience the day tomorrow as you would like it to be, with smooth flow and solutions for the whole. Finish by sitting in bed and saying to yourself: "Many thanks for a fantastic day with smooth flow and solutions for the whole."
- Lie down and go to sleep without counting out.

### Example of using the Nightfilm technique

**The Day Today**: I talked with my son and he told me that he'd be taking two exams. I became frustrated when I talked to a supplier who was so busy with everything else that we would have to wait. I feel like I'm coming down with the flu. I need to clear up project X, which isn't running as smoothly as it should. My boss wasn't very understanding when I presented my plan. It felt very unfair when... (here I empty all of my feelings and emotions).

**The Day Tomorrow**: I wake up and feel refreshed, healthy and at peace. I groom myself and travel to work. My son phones, and I feel happy when he tells me that he made top grades on both exams. The supplier came by with flowers and apologized for behaving so badly. Everything is arranged for the delivery, and he promised to give us a good discount. My boss came by my office and invited me to lunch. He had thought over my plan and was sorry that he had not immediately seen what a good idea it is. The project is flowing smoothly and everything is done. I'm sitting in bed and it's late in the evening. Many thanks for a fantastic day with smooth flow and solutions for the whole.

### Another example of using the Nightfilm technique

**The Day Today:** (There isn't always a lot to write about. It depends on what we do and who we are. If we don't have anything to write about, then look around you to see if there is a project or someone else who needs your help).

**The Day Tomorrow:** I wake up and feel refreshed, healthy and in peace. I travel to the airport, where my plane is on time. We land 10 minutes ahead of schedule and XX picks me up for a meeting. We cooperate very well, smiling and feeling that we find solutions for the whole by working together. I get a ride to my hotel and enjoy a quiet evening. I'm now sitting in bed and it's late evening. Many thanks for a fantastic day with smooth flow and solutions for the whole.

# With good intentions and the right focus you can do just about anything

"Freedom is not worth having if it doesn't include freedom to make mistakes"

—Mahatma Gandhi (1869–1948)

*You say that our intentions regarding what we do and what we want to change, are the basis for everything that we do. Can you explain that more thoroughly?*

Intention is the driving force to get where you want to go, and a good intention strengthens Delta, presence of mind and connectedness. The word intention comes from the Latin word *intendere*, to intend, and in this context it means being attentive and complete. Complete for me means connection to a greater universal community. My motivation for what I do is therefore important for me. It should benefit not only me, but also a greater community. I believe that a good intention is the steering factor for attaining a magical daily life.

A good intention comes from the heart, the creative inner, and not from the will, the physical outer. That means, for example, that we cannot use the ESP sense to snoop around in the lives of others.

*Isn't that something that we humans fear, Deborah?*

Yes, and that's why I mentioned "snooping around." Many people have asked me: "Deborah, if you teach people to use the ESP sense, aren't you afraid that they will come 'visiting' and spy on your life?" No, I'm not afraid of that, because you need to have a good intention when you use your ESP sense, or you will not receive correct information. That has been tried and tested. We cannot interfere with the lives of others if they don't want us to.

*Can the techniques you teach be used in a negative way, for example to harm rivals or to obtain information that someone doesn't want you to have?*

If your intention is to harm another person, you are no longer in the creative state. Then you are "above the surface," on top of the iceberg. Some have said to me that they believe they can be harmed, or they're afraid of being harmed. Then it's not others who are harming you, but your own thoughts that someone will harm you, that influence your body. I remember a woman who participated in a course many years ago. She had tried to give someone a headache, but ended up with a headache herself.

We humans have an ego while in Gamma, Beta, Alpha and Theta, but it disappears in Delta. It is therefore important for me to train people to seek out the ego-free zone, where questions like this don't even come up.

This fear that some have about someone obtaining information that they don't want to share, is pointless. What do we have to hide?

When we work with self-development in a conscious manner and gain access to greater insight, we have nothing to hide, and the question becomes irrelevant.

Yes, you may get information, but if you use it in a negative way then you only harm yourself. You may also receive incorrect information, and your imagination can spin around that and create things that aren't good for you. When you work in a goal-oriented manner for self-development, it means that you are responsible for your own life, are most concerned with that, and stop bothering so much about the lives of others.

A good intention is about more than you alone, it's not based on ego, but on wholeness. When one has a good intention, one treats others with respect. Norwegians are familiar with the "Law of Cardamom Town" from a Norwegian tale by Torbjørn Egner: "You shouldn't bother others, you should be nice and kind, otherwise you can do as you like."

First you need to find your good intention—what do you want? Then you focus on what you want. Thereafter use your ESP sense to help understand what steps to take, and follow up by taking the steps towards what you want.

*There's a saying that "The will steers the works." Is that what you mean?*
For me that is completely wrong. The will is above the surface, on top of the iceberg. Much more is needed.

*Come on! If someone wants something badly enough, won't that help?*
Yes, but the will is controlled by the rational left brain hemisphere. You also need the right brain hemisphere to gain insight about why you want it so much. Is it due to a need for recognition, fame, wealth, happiness? What is the motivation behind the will? The will and your intention must be coherent, or you will not arrive at your goal.

*So you're saying that intention and intuition must work together?*
Exactly! In addition you must learn to focus. Then you reach your goal.

*What a chore! We can focus, if we must! Do you mean that's also something we need to learn?*

Definitely. We humans are very unfocused. Our thoughts wander everywhere, and our minds are filled with many things. Then we lose sight of what we want to attract.

*What do you mean now?*

I'll give some examples that many might recognize. I remember the very first car I bought. I had earned some money on a stock option and finally could afford to buy a car. I went to a dealer, and he had a nice Mazda 323 in a very special blue color. I hadn't seen that color before, and I decided to buy the car. From that instant I noticed many Mazda 323's with exactly the same color.

I have three children. Every time I was pregnant, it seemed as though everyone else had chosen the same time to have a child. Women with bulging shapes everywhere I looked, and baby carriages in every direction I turned.

These are examples of how we attract whatever we focus upon, although not consciously. Some call it the "Law of Attraction." We must, therefore, learn to focus consciously on what we want, in order to attract just that.

# Assignment for the sixth week

In addition to the basic exercise for relaxation and the Nightfilm, this week you are to learn to register unwanted thoughts, and shift your focus with the help of intention.

It's important to take control of your imagination and thoughts, and this training will help you to hold the right focus for reaching your goals and smooth flow.

### Exercise 6: Intention and focus

- Pay attention throughout your day, and come to a halt if you have thoughts or feelings you do not want.
- Choose an affirmation that suits you.
- Take a deep breath and consciously change your thoughts.
- Repeat the affirmation to yourself for 90 seconds so that the feeling has time to establish itself in your body, before you continue what you are doing. Use your watch to measure the seconds.

# What does self-development really mean?

"Everyone wants to change humanity, but no one wants to change themselves"
—Leo Tolstoy (1828–1910)

*There are about as many definitions of self-development as there are courses and books on the subject. Does it need to be so difficult?*

No. As you know, I like to keep things simple. Self-development means developing oneself. Few think about the fact that self-development is the development that we go through every single day, either deliberately and consciously—or without being aware. Whether we work for self-development or not, development happens, because everything is constantly changing. When we begin working with self-development, it becomes deliberate and conscious. When you realize that you've become entangled on a sub-conscious level, you can untangle yourself.

*Yes, many of us are better at self-entanglement than self-development?*

Exactly! I previously developed myself together with everyone else, but not very consciously at all. I tagged along with everyone else and allowed myself to be steered by truths and the refrain of a pop song that "life is sad and unfair."

After I took charge of my own development, I became aware that I am in control and can control the part of my iceberg that steers. I decide, not anyone else.

I am the only one who can decide how I should develop, and the same applies for you. Then life begins to be thrilling. In my experience, life has a meaning. I can participate in life, have a lovely life, steer my life and decide the direction. I can use my tools to cope with whatever I meet along the way. Although we begin conscious and deliberate self-development, we can still meet challenges that we must be able to handle. New challenges come along all the time, and it helps to have tools at hand to deal with them and take over the helm of our own ship.

*My son is wise for his age. One one day I jokingly said to him: "Since you know the answer for everything, what is the meaning of life?" He looked solemnly at me and said "The meaning of life is to give life meaning." That left me speechless.*

That was well said! I often hear people say, "Oh well, there must be a reason for that." To me that's only a poor excuse and a defense for something that we don't understand consciously. It's not useful to just go along with development without understanding what one is doing, and without realizing that we in fact can change it.

*Those were strong words!*

Yes, but I dare to say it, for that is exactly what I used to do. "Yes, there must be a reason for that; I'll understand it someday."

No wonder the world is in the state it's in, when we accept that way of thinking.

I often quote Leo Tolstoy: "Everyone wants to change humanity, but no one wants to change themselves."

Many resist change, and by that I mean unconscious resistance, not conscious. The tip of the iceberg is the conscious part of ourselves, while resistance lies under the surface and is the part that steers. The part that is below the surface makes up about 90 percent of each of us. There is so little that we are consciously aware of. This can be very frustrating when we consciously desire change, but fail to bring it about.

*What can we do about that?*

We must become aware of the truths we have stored within, and that some of them may not always serve us. That is why it's often easy to get started with deliberate self-development, but also easy to give up.

Change always starts with an acknowledgement or realization. Sometimes this is painful, and it may be so hard to bear that we retreat and lose sight of our goal. The pain is often short lived, however. Short-term pain for long-term gain.

Today we know that mental training results in physiological changes in the brain. That's why it's important to keep our focus on our goal and remember why we want change.

Deliberate and conscious choices mean that I make the choices myself!

During all the years after I was ill, I actively worked with myself and my own self-development. This has opened many amazing doors.

I've created a list of elements needed for self-development that I've used as a template for my own development. These elements have been important, even decisive, for me.

The first element is becoming aware of my own thoughts, words and actions. This was a difficult process for me. I became depressed and somewhat discouraged. When I started taking notice of my own thoughts, I began to realize that the kinesiologist who had said that I had much negativity in me, was in fact right.

*How exactly did you notice that?*

I noticed how judgmental I was when I met other people. It was almost tragic. It can be a tough process to realize how much negativity is in one's own mind. I judged how people dressed, what they said and how they spoke, as well as how they coped with things. What did I get more of when I was doing that? A judgmental life that was definitely not a good one.

*Ouch, I recognize myself there. I was sometimes exactly like that. No matter how hard I judged others, I was even harder towards myself. It was a vicious circle that was difficult to break out of.*

Yes, I understand, but first we must become aware, so don't be discouraged. You might not hold as much negativity as I did, but you may discover some things about yourself that can be uncomfortable. It's important to remember that what you have in your mind, in your thoughts and in your consciousness, is in fact what you attract to yourself in life.

Think back to what we said in the chapter about truths—the magnet that either attracted or repelled—for in a good life the two ends of the magnet must work together. The part that repels or sends out is the conscious and the part that attracts is the subconscious. Thoughts, words and actions arise based on the subconscious. That creates our attitudes. We learn, and are good students!

*You're talking about the wholeness that we all are a part of?*

Right. What everyone else does with their life, what others are or are not, is also about you. If you have an opinion about others, that tells something about you. We must care about others without judging them.

We judge others because that is what we learned. We think that it's all about others. What others do, what others say, what kind of car they drive, what kind of house they live in, what their husband or wife is like. It's easy for us to find ourselves thinking "will that relationship last?"

All the while, we must also remember to not take personally all that we have stored within that we have not chosen ourselves. Our attitude must be: "OK, let me take a look at what is within me, perhaps doing that can help me in my life."

If you want to change your life, this is one of the most important things for you to do. Your thoughts, words and actions create your life.

*Being so concerned about others and what they do, think and mean, is something we have with us from childhood?*

Yes. At the courses for children and teens we see that attitudes are formed at a very early stage, and they are with us the rest of our lives at the subconscious level. These hidden attitudes can create a lot of discomfort in our adult lives. That's why it's so important for me that we do something about it, and teach children about this while they are young. I've decided that before I leave this planet, this is going to be a subject in schools. If I had known about this when I was young, my life would have been different. I could have avoided creating a lot of muck in life. Sorry about that expression, but this subject is very important for me.

*When we feel so strongly about this, the positive effect is even greater when we do manage to develop ourselves in the right direction?*

I've experienced that myself! I quickly noticed a change in my life when I became aware of my attitudes. Just think about envy and jealousy. "Don't be so positive, Deborah! You say that you are so well off, Deborah," some folks say while giving me a sour look. I think this is the most widespread epidemic we have, and such thoughts corrode our bodies. It isn't possible to be happy if life is full of envy and jealousy. Again, I speak from experience. If you want to experience smooth flow and a good life, you must change such feelings, and you are the only one who can do that. Everyone is better off when we feel joy for the success of others.

*With this as a background, then acknowledging follows naturally?*

Acknowledgement is the next element. Merely acknowledging that we realize something is enough to create a change in itself. It starts movement, like ripples in the water. We must take the first step before anything can happen. Often we don't take the first step. We say: "I want that, I want it to be that way," but it's a little scary, so we stand there, unable to act. Change is often accompanied by fear. What do we meet? The *unknown*, and then we become insecure. We stay in the same place, even if that place is not a good place to be.

Doors start opening as soon as we take the first step, and on the other side of those doors we will see things that we hadn't thought possible.

*But it's not so easy?*

No. Acknowledgement is one of the most difficult parts of the self-development process. Think about the left brain hemisphere picking up information from the file drawer—something old, and it sees only one folder at a time. That's why we so often hold onto our own truths. We have in addition learned that we must be right, and the combination of these two stops development. We need to be able to see a greater wholeness, and acknowledgement comes from the right brain hemisphere that is able to see the whole picture.

I've had to acknowledge an awful lot in my life, and although it's been difficult at times, I would happily do it all over again because I know about the doors that have been opened for me.

The good thing about acknowledgement is that we can move on, and use the new insight to influence our surroundings in a more positive way. However, in order to find motivation and inspiration in life, we must set goals. That is another important element in self-development; without goals we don't get anywhere.

*You point out that people themselves are responsible in this process. They must do it themselves; no one else can do it for them.*

Yes, that is a fundamental element. I—Deborah—steer my own life. Everything I see in the physical dimension comes from deep within me. I must then take responsibility for doing unto others as I would like them to do unto me. I must speak to others as I want them to speak to me. I must *be* all that I want to see in my life. If I see something I don't like, I must take responsibility and do something within myself.

We are merely humans on this path, so we are bound to make blunders. These are experiences that we gather, and we go on to make amends.

When I started the self-development process and started taking responsibility for myself, which also meant taking care of myself, people around me said: "Are you going to be completely selfish now, only thinking about yourself?"

Wrong. I've never helped so many people as I have after I started my own self-development. By that I mean help them, not do it for them. Today I use all of my time to help others while also helping myself. If I am not well, then I influence others in an undesirable way, and I'm not able to do anything for them either. We all need to update the "server," so that others may get good ideas about the insight we've learned.

*I've also experienced this in my development. The more I put my own life in order, the more I can be there for others. But we must also set limits. Isn't that a dilemma, or even a restriction?*

Setting limits is also an important element, and a very scary one for some. We often express ourselves more strongly than we should. If I work within myself to feel secure when I speak my mind, and be myself, I will be able to say what I mean in a good way; be able to feel and think without fear. I experience being able to set limits as liberating and creative, not limiting.

I have, for example, had to work with setting limits regarding how I allow people to treat me. My iceberg contained truths about abuse, and I was used to people treating me that way. I had to change that belief within myself while at the same time beginning to say to others that this was no longer accepted. Not until then could I reject that truth.

*People who work with disadvantaged children, often say that the absence of limits is a contributing cause to many problems?*

I've also heard that. When you set limits in a nice way for yourself, you become a more secure adult and will set good limits where necessary.

I believe that everyone needs two things in childhood to get a good start in life: clear limits and unconditional love. This seems to me to be two sides of the same matter.

*"Must I forgive?" many ask, and have difficulty doing that. You have experienced much injustice. Have you really forgiven all those who have hurt you?*

We don't forgive the actions, just the people behind them. Yes, I have forgiven everyone along the way. My grandmother was an important inspiration for me. She always told me not to hold grudges towards anyone. "You see, little one, they don't understand what they've done," she said to me.

Forgiveness has been necessary for me, and is another important element of self-development. If I had continued to carry the feeling of resentment with me, I wouldn't be alive today. Resentment, hate, and grudges lie in our subconscious and gnaw away at us. Since thoughts and what is stored in the subconscious influence the body, we must forgive in order to be free.

We've unfortunately learned that some things are unforgiveable. If that is one of your truths, it will just keep accumulating and you will attract additional negative incidents. No one wants that.

It may seem difficult and painful, but learn to forgive and I can assure you that amazing doors will open.

Everyone is built in the same way, with a conscious and a subconscious part. Behind every tragedy lies the tragedy of another person. We don't do things to be evil, but based on learned truths.

By learning to know oneself, you will be able to see other people without condemnation. Then one forgives. For me it was even more difficult to forgive myself than to forgive people who had hurt me. I carried a lot of feelings of guilt within me, since I thought that things that happened were my fault. Guilt is also something that has been learned, and the word should be deleted from the dictionary.

It feels magical to be free from feelings of resentment and guilt. It's absolutely something I recommend, and this is a key factor for attaining freedom and inner peace. With inner peace we begin to see peace all around us as well, and the dream of a more peaceful planet is then within reach.

*It sounds like much of this is about trusting that it will eventually have an effect and help me to be a better person?*

What you say there, reminds me of something I've heard, that the difference between faith and superstition is the number of people who have faith. It's not exactly like that, but yes, we need to trust and have faith that the process we are going through, is the path and life itself. This is also an important element. Sometimes I say that I *trust* the life process, and I've borrowed a story from a good friend and colleague, Børre Nyborg. His grandfather was from an island in northern Norway and had many good stories. I've taken the liberty to change the story a little.

It's about an old woman who walks home from church one Sunday with the pastor. The going is slow because the old woman has trouble with her legs. They come to a suspension bridge that they must cross. The old woman is afraid, and the pastor says: "Remember your faith and trust that you are protected and well taken care of."

"Yes, of course I believe," she said, and for each step she takes he can hear her say "I believe." Everything is fine until she gets halfway over the bridge, then she falls through an opening, and while falling she could be heard to call out: "That's what I believed would happen!"

Something one can learn from that story is that it's easier to trust that you can cope with things that you meet if you have trust in life and yourself.

*We must also be patient. Patience is a virtue, isn't that so?*

Yes, patience is another element, and it's the first word I write on the board when I teach a course. To remind participants to take one step at a time.

It's difficult to perceive correct information with our ESP sense if we are stressed, and impatience makes us feel stressed.

My friend Børre uses an expression from northern Norway that says something about how important it is to take your time: "The dog waits until the food cools down." This means that even a dog has enough sense to be patient and wait for the food to cool, so it doesn't get burned. He has also discovered that a lack of patience with himself is a cunning way to exercise self-criticism.

Let's say it this way: I don't think he's the only one that comes to such a conclusion, for the first step on the way to patience is to find it in oneself.

I've worked a lot with that, and even tipped over in the other direction—I became too patient. When we're too patient we can deprive others from learning experiences, in that they are not held responsible. I've also met people who think they know what's best for everyone else, because they themselves have gained insight.

Don't judge others because they don't see what you see. We have different truths stored under the surface in our iceberg, and we must first of all be responsible for our own life. Remember that everything needs to be in balance.

---

### Elements of self-development

When I feel that my life has stagnated or is not flowing as smoothly as I would like, I use this list of elements to see if one or more of them can give me a clue about what I need to work on:

- Increasing awareness
- Acknowledgement
- Goals
- Responsibility for own life
- Setting limits in a good way

- Transformation
- Forgiveness
- Trust
- Patience

The elements are the process.
The process is life itself.
Life is NOW!

# Assignment for the seventh week

This week is reserved for increasing awareness. In addition, you are to continue writing a Nightfilm every evening so that it becomes a habit. I also recommend that you do the basic exercise for relaxation three times this week. You may do it more often if you like.

One of the elements of self-development is becoming aware of words, thoughts and actions. As we mentioned earlier, thoughts influence the body, both the conscious ones and those that are stored in the subconscious. What do we think about during our daily lives? Do we get annoyed? Are we frustrated?

When you've read all the chapters in this book, you will see that you can use what you've learned to adjust, change and understand all that you have become aware of this week.

### Exercise 7: Increasing awareness

- Make note of episodes during the course of the day where you lose energy and get tired or in a bad mood.
- What happens to you?
- What thoughts or incidents provoked you to lose energy, become tired or in a bad mood?
- When you've written it down, take a deep breath and shift your focus to something positive before you go on with your day.

# Visions and goals

"The problems of the world cannot possibly be solved by skeptics or cynics whose horizons are limited by obvious realities. We need men and women who can dream of things that never were..."
—John F. Kennedy (1917–1963)

*You work with goal-oriented self-development. I didn't realize that self-development had anything to do with goals. Please explain, Deborah.*

It's very logical for me. If you don't know where you're going, then it's pretty difficult to get there. It's easy for us to fall into a pattern of living someone else's dream, instead of our own. It's therefore important to have your own dreams to work towards.

To me, the word vision means a dream that we can stretch towards. I've been in companies where they had no visions, only goals. That means that there's nothing to stretch towards. If we stop dreaming, then we stop growing as humans.

I'll therefore give you some examples of visions. Among others, I have a vision about peace.

*I think you're not alone about that, but does it make sense for "ordinary people" like us to go around with such unreachable goals?*

Many people think that way, but the reason I have this as a vision is that I know who I was before my deliberate and conscious self-development started, and I know who I am today. If I could change so much in myself and become peaceful within, then everyone else can as well. That's why it's realistic for us to stretch towards peace. The reason I share so much is that I want to contribute to creating a more peaceful planet Earth.

*Can you give us an example of a more tangible vision?*

Yes. We've had some courses for pre-school employees. A vision for a pre-school might be to provide conditions that create confident adults.

*What about personal visions?*

"I live a good life, and each day is magical" is the vision I use in order to show how we can continue working.

*You like to quote JFK, who said that skeptics and cynics limit their horizon. Explain!*

Limitations happen when we only use our left brain hemisphere. To create something new, we must dream about it. That means including creativity and wholeness, as the right brain hemisphere does. Think of the iceberg. The very small part that's above the surface is often what we use as the basis for our decisions. That part also contains all that we should do, could do, and should have done. All of this is very limiting for us and our future. If we look at the solutions that often are chosen in different areas, we can quickly confirm that many of them are not long term, good solutions for the whole. They are patched up and patched up until we have complete chaos.

*This is where the Nightfilm comes in?*

Using the Nightfilm gives us access to all information without any limits whatsoever. Thereafter we must set goals and use The Creative Corner to stay on course and do whatever is necessary. We must set goals and take action, not just let things happen or wonder what will happen.

I know how limited I was. I previously believed only what I could see. My education as an economist was limited by obvious realities.

In addition, I had learned as a young child that I shouldn't wish for anything. If I pestered my father for something, he'd say: "Spit in one hand and make a wish in the other, and see which hand gets most." As the child I was, I did as he said. There was always most spit, and I quickly learned that it was no use to wish for anything.

The same applied to using my will. "Your will, my girl, lies in my apron pocket," my mother would say as she patted her apron pocket. I grew up in an age where mothers had aprons with large pockets, so my will remained there until long after I was an adult. Mothers and fathers mean no harm when they say such things. My parents had also learned these expressions and passed them on, as good parents do.

Not to mention deserving something. That's also something we learn when we're very young. We must do something to deserve getting something. All of this lies under the surface as indisputable truths, and prevents us from setting good goals for ourselves.

*So where should one start?*

When we set a goal we must ask ourselves what it is that *I* want, and not what everyone else wants—for that is quite irrelevant for you to become the whole person you are meant to be. Small goals give small results, and large goals give large results. You must begin where it is natural for you.

*I'm interested in tennis, and remember well the story about how the tennis genius Björn Borg started his career. His father won a racket at a tombola when Björn was three or four years old. From that day on he stood and hit a tennis ball against the garage door for several hours a day. It probably wasn't so nice for his parents and the neighbors, but one must admire his resolve! By the way, shouldn't one consider others in this process?*

Yes, of course, but you must start with yourself. I believe that in order to get a comprehensive picture of solutions and dreams, you need to look within in order to communicate with the whole, where you are a part of a community. Remember what we said about the network and the server.

*What are the greatest challenges in the goal process?*

Many feel that it's difficult to write down their goals. "What if someone else reads it, and I must be responsible for reaching it? What if I don't reach the goal, confirming the truth that I can't accomplish anything? What if I really accomplish the goal? What will people say then?" We are afraid of the comments and envy of others, unfortunately. Somewhere inside us we all desire to be liked by others. "What if I don't want to reach that goal after all?" Well, then you can remember that everything is constantly changing, also your goals. It's OK to change your mind, to change your goal. That is natural.

Many are used to setting goals at work, but not in their private lives. Perhaps it should be the other way around, since the private, personal goals are more important. How I feel also influences my work. If I have troubles in my private life, then I'm not well off at work either, even when I put on a smiling mask.

All company leaders are served well by helping their employees find a good life. It gives them much joy, and will be reflected in results for the company as well. Less sick leave and greater efficiency gives better returns.

Goals are not set with the mind alone, but also with the heart, in order to achieve the best possible whole. What I want, the desires that I radiate outwards, must be in agreement with the attracting part that lies within me.

# Using a goal journal

"The secret of getting ahead is getting started. The secret of getting started is breaking your complex, overwhelming tasks into small manageable tasks, and then starting on the first one"
—Mark Twain (1835–1910)

*Mark Twain understood that, but can you make it even more simple for us ordinary people?*

When we set goals, we tend to think so much about all that needs to be done, all that we think we cannot do, and everything that we're afraid of, that we lose a lot of energy before we've even started. We become unable to act. That's why it will help to take the advice of Mark Twain about breaking your tasks down and taking one step at a time.

In addition to a book for your Nightfilms, I recommend that you keep a journal where you write all of your goals and visions. You can enjoy pleasant moments leafing through your goal journal, as if you're with a friend.

One vision might be: *I live a good life, and each day is magical.*

Formulate your goals and visions as if they already have happened, as if you are there. Begin by defining "what is a good life for me?"

Note your vision on the first page of your goal journal. This is what you will stretch towards.

On the next page, write "What is a good life for me?" Then write a list of items that represent things that you believe are important for a good life. For example:

- Work
- Home
- Health
- Family
- Friends
- Hobbies

*That seems reasonable and logical. What's the next step?*

When your list is ready, turn to the next page and write the first item at the top of the page. In this example it's work. Ask yourself: What kind of job do I feel would be a good job for me, a job that helps me to achieve the goal of a good life? What do I like to do? What would I like to do if I listen to my heart, and not just my mind? Continue with additional questions.

These questions may generate new goals for you. Perhaps you would like a different position, or to study? Divide each goal into manageable tasks.

*Can you give us an example?*

Yes indeed. Let's take hobbies. I need to start by asking the question: What do I like to do? I love music and enjoy singing in a chorus. What kind of chorus? Well, when I was young I sang in a Ten Sing choir. That's for younger people. Perhaps a gospel choir, with happy songs on the program? I'd like to sing in a gospel choir for adults, but there's no such choir in the area where I live. Then my goal can be to start such a gospel choir.

*What would the tasks be?*

I could go to the local newspaper and ask them to help me. Perhaps they could write something about it. There must be more people who would like to sing in a gospel choir for adults.

I would also need a conductor who would like to do this in their spare time. Perhaps I can find him or her through the local paper as well.

*OK. But how do we proceed when the goals are written down and we're going to start working on the tasks?*

Include the goals you've decided on in your Nightfilm, that you have already learned to use. This is important for smooth flow and ideal solutions on the way to your goal.

In addition, you are to use The Creative Corner for goals. The procedure is described in the next exercise. I explain that in Step 2 you are to invite an advisor or expert in this area.

*What's the idea behind that?*

It's easier for our left brain hemisphere to cooperate when it has something physical to relate to, and it's easier for us to be unbiased. That means that you're to invite someone that you believe to be an expert in the area we're considering.

Another reason that I created the technique this way, is that we need confirmation. When we get an idea, we want to share it with others. We need to become more self-secure, and this technique helps. If you use the tools you learn in this book, you'll also receive comprehensive solutions and ideas from the "server." Ideas that you then must follow through and implement.

# Assignment for the eighth week

In addition to writing a Nightfilm in the evening, this week you are to work with goals. Write your visions and goals in a goal journal, and take plenty of time to think about what a good life is for you, and what goals you need in order to get there.

Use The Creative Corner for goals, and work your way through your goals this week.

It's important that you take seriously any ideas and thoughts that occur to you in your daily life, and that you follow up on them by taking action. Most ideas appear as thoughts while you're awake in your daily life. Don't disregard them.

### Exercise 8: The Creative Corner for goals

- Close your eyes and count down from 7 to 1. Now you only need to take a deep breath at each number. When you've reached number 1, assume that you are in your inner room, and that you are in The Creative Corner.
- **Step 1:** Think through your present situation and find out where you are in relation to the goal you've decided on.
- **Step 2:** Invite an advisor or expert in the area you are thinking about, and conduct an inner conversation with this person. Consider ideas about what can help you to reach your goal, and ideas about what you must do. When you are finished, thank your advisor for helping. It may seem as if you're talking to yourself, and that is natural.
- **Step 3:** Describe your goal, and include any ideas that came to you in Step 2. Specify details.
- **Step 4:** Imagine that you are living the final result that you've created for your goal. Listen to what you hear, smell fragrances you recognize, observe colors and register how it feels—as if you already have achieved your goal. This step is important for setting your goal in motion.

When you want to end the session, use the procedure for counting out as described in Exercise 1. If new ideas have come to you, then write them down in your goal journal.

# Improve communication
# with yourself and others

"I cannot find happiness anywhere,
unless I can find it within myself"
—Edvard Grieg (1843–1907)

*Much of your course is about communication with others and within ourselves. Why is this so fundamental?*

All subjects that we talk about in this book are parts that need to be considered in order to understand communication with ourselves, with others, and with a whole. Communication means transfer of information.

While growing up we learn things that become truths for us. These truths become stored in the part of our iceberg that is under the surface. While stored there, they make up the attracting part of the magnet, so we might say: More of what I already have within me, comes to me.

When I gained this insight, it saved my life. For me it has become quite logical that if I want something in my life that is different from what I already have, I must go deep into my iceberg to bring forth whatever is there, and then change it.

*Now I understand the course participant who wondered if this is a new law of nature.*

I believe that we are built that way. That means that when things come to a halt, I need to look for answers and solutions within myself. As Grieg said: "I cannot find happiness anywhere, unless I can find it within myself."

I previously thought that I could search for good fortune and joy somewhere outside of myself. I had learned that others make you happy, others can make you smile, others can help you. Yes, but not in the long term.

If you find joy within yourself, it will be lasting joy. No one will be able to disturb your serenity. Nothing can be taken from you when you own the feeling within yourself. When this way of thinking becomes integrated, you will always be able to find that good feeling within yourself again, even when you encounter something that temporarily disturbs you.

*So it's not possible to be happy without beginning within yourself? Many of us define happiness in relation to things that are outside of ourselves: "meeting the right one," becoming wealthy, getting a better job, etc.*

I think you're right about that. We're good at defining ourselves according to what others think about us and from outer circumstances. If I meet something in life that I don't like, something that disturbs or upsets me, it's important for me to stop and ask myself what my magnet is attracting. Why did I meet someone who was in a bad mood or angry? Why is my project being held up? Why am I losing enthusiasm and energy now? Why am I encountering this?

I've been working like this for many years, and it's saved my life. Coming across something that's negative doesn't mean that I'm not good enough. It simply means that something has been stored in my subconscious which is attracting it. If I am experiencing negative flow, I can find the reason within myself, make changes and thereby enjoy positive, smooth flow again.

*That sounds like the kind of statement that causes fuses to blow for a lot of people. The kind of thing that gets them to groan about anything called "self-development" and close their ears.*

Of course I can understand that. I remember when I first heard about this way of thinking. I was furious, for the first thing that came to mind was: "So it's my own fault that I was raped twice while I was still a child and was sexually abused by others as well? and *I* am the one who's supposed to do something about it? Unfair! Unjust!" We have strong truths buried within us regarding fault and guilt.

You might as well swallow it and take a deep breath. We function in this way whether we like it or not. When one has found inner insight and acknowledgement, life can resume its smooth flow. Some call it the Law of the Universe, the Law of Attraction or The Secret—it doesn't matter what we call it, as long as we do something about it.

*I think you need to further explain that. Is it my fault if I meet someone who is angry at work tomorrow?*

If I meet someone who is angry, it doesn't necessarily mean that I'm angry, but it may tell me something else. This could be due to any number of things stored within me. If I've grown up with much anger around me, then I will attract more of that. This gives me an opportunity to set limits for what I'll accept, if I've become aware and acknowledged what is stored within me. It can also mean that I am carrying anger around with me, and I'll then have an opportunity to do something about that. There might also be individual episodes that prevent me from achieving what I want. So using The Creative Corner to transform will open up for something new in my life.

I was stuck in many emotions. I felt sorry for myself, I was envious of others because they had more than I had—I suffered from many syndromes, as I call them: Self-pity syndrome, envy syndrome, jealousy syndrome and helpfulness syndrome, to name a few. This is very damaging. We all have this syndrome to some degree, so it's best to just walk past that point in order to see how we function as humans and not be upset because we function as we do.

*I can understand that self-pity, envy and jealousy are negative syndromes, but what about helpfulness? Isn't that positive?*

The helpfulness syndrome isn't any better than any other. Yes, we should help, and "the greatest joy you can have, is making other people happy," as it's often said. That's right, but only if your intention is good. If you are helping in order to appear to be a nice girl or boy, or because you want attention and to be seen, or for other reasons, then the help you give is only damaging. Damaging because you are not genuine; the help you give is not from the heart. If you help with a smile that is not a smile in your subconscious, you are in reality sending out bad vibrations that don't help anyone.

*You've told me that these syndromes can be so damaging that they can result in physical symptoms?*

Yes, I developed migraine headaches for that reason. I felt I needed to be a nice girl and help, not always because I really wanted to. Subconsciously we will then find ways to avoid this, and in my case it was migraines. Then I could say with good conscience: "Sorry, I can't because I've got a migraine." If there was a party that I didn't really want to go to, I got a migraine. This is of course not a good way to say no—in bed with the shades drawn for three days. This is not something that happens deliberately and consciously, but comes from the part of the iceberg that steers. I've worked a lot with this syndrome, and today I can say that I'm glad to help when I really mean it, or say no, sorry, at other times. In that way I can help in a good way. Do you recognize what I'm talking about?

*Yes, I must admit that I do, although I haven't had physical symptoms. I had to have a showdown with myself a while back. I realized that I was motivated a little too much by a need for a "pat on the back." The result was that I was very busy measuring my placement in relation to my colleagues and how I might appear to be better than them, and so on. I was often angry and aggressive, and wasn't happy with myself.*

It was like that for me too. In the beginning of my self-development I had thoughts like "enough is enough," and pulled the covers up over my head. It was just that it didn't get any better with my head under the covers, so that didn't help. At other times I thought: "stop the world, I want to get off!" but that didn't work either. So what was left? I had to make a choice. How do I want things to be? It was necessary to dig in once again. Pull yourself together, persevere and never give up.

*Can you give us a concrete example?*

Let's say that I'm in a meeting at work and a colleague says something that I feel frustrated about. I even lose energy, the wind goes out of my sails. What's happening?

To begin with, this is a subconscious reaction. That is, a reaction that comes from some truth that is stored in my subconscious. Perhaps a word, the way something was said, or body language from my colleague that sets off a memory that my subconscious recognizes. My brain remembers something that it has seen, heard or felt earlier. If I'm not aware of my communication with others, I'll create chaos in a case like this.

In order to change that negative reaction to smooth flow, I must find the cause. I use The Creative Corner to find the cause and then transform it.

What happens then? Next time I'm in a similar situation I won't react in the same way, because my inner truth has been transformed.

*OK, so I can change things within myself, but can I help others?*

Yes, we can work to help ourselves and others. We can't do the work for others, but we can be of help. Just the fact that I put things right within myself also influences others around me. That is the greatest discovery I've made. When I take responsibility for transforming painful feelings within me, it also has an effect in the world around me.

Everyone can experience poor relations with another person. It might be a neighbor, a boss, a sibling or parents. Using these tools you have an opportunity to make amends. Life is too short to throw it away on things that only bring unhappiness. Maintaining feelings of hate or resentment don't help you, your body or anyone else. That's why forgiveness is an important element of self-development.

There's a lot stored within us that influences our communication, and if we don't know what's there, then we won't understand why people react the way they do to what we say. We go around feeling misunderstood. We bring this into relationships. We argue, and hostility arises. I've had to work a lot to find out where my communication really comes from. For example: Why are the things I communicate interpreted differently than I want them to be?

*That reminds me of the politician who a few years ago expressed displeasure with the voters who didn't vote for him. He "wanted other voters."*

Yes, it's a common reaction to think that way, instead of looking within to find out what oneself is communicating that gets others to misunderstand the message.

*When you stand before people as often as you do, Deborah, and are to teach them how to live their lives…*

I don't tell anyone how to live their lives. I give them tools they can use, so they can live their own lives and not the lives of everyone else.

*Yes, but what I was coming to was that it's natural that those you meet will examine you and your life very carefully, because you—whether you want to or not—stand there as an example of someone who has "made it" in your life. How does that feel?*

It's natural that people would like to have someone to look up to. However, I say very clearly that I'm not looking for disciples or admiration. That's quite far from what I want. My life has included much pain and difficulty—violence and abuse, conflicts, broken relationships and illness.

What I've accomplished, after much trying and failing, is to be happy no matter what I encounter! *That* is what I would like to teach. If one manages that, then one is prepared to cope with anything that comes along in life.

*That's what I like about your courses. You always give examples from your own life and your own reality. As you say, you've been through a lot of drama throughout the years.*

Hmmm. Right now someone in my family is seriously ill, and my finances are very tight because I use all my resources on the new courses and the research project that I'm very dedicated to. But I'm happy within because I use my tools to cope with whatever comes along.

I do this without burdening people around me with my problems. For me, happiness is what I make of each and every day, not money, the "man in my life" or other isolated factors.

*You sometimes use a hot-air balloon as an image related to improving one's own communication?*

Yes, I feel it's a good metaphor. Imagine that the hot-air balloon is your life, and you're sitting in the basket under the balloon. You have a number of sandbags attached to the basket that hold the balloon on the ground. The sandbags are your inner "truths", the learned statements that prevent you from rising upwards. Some of them must be thrown overboard in order to get started. Then you have the flame that warms up the air and causes the balloon to rise. That is your intention, the driving force behind thoughts and action. It's necessary to get everything going. And you need to rise up in the sky in order to get a better overview!

*Some of our inner truths must be positive? We can't throw them all overboard, because the balloon would rise so high that it would crack open!*

You need some sandbags, of course. But you need to get rid of those that prevent smooth flow in your life. Again, this is about balance.

# Differences between masculine and feminine communication

*I have the impression that it's easier for women than for men to accept what you teach at your courses. What do you think about that?*

In many ways it's been difficult for me to communicate with men. My father was authoritarian, a doctor abused me, male bosses have been in charge of steering me. Fear of men has been a large part of my life. I've also experienced much injustice. More than once I've had great ideas and thoughts that have been "stolen" by a man. I've attracted people who needed help and who I have helped, who later point a finger of accusation at me and say I'm guilty of one thing or another.

Communication between people has become extremely important for me. The more I've worked with things that have happened to me, the more I've understood how I communicate myself.

I've learned an enormous amount and had "a-ha" experiences again and again during the past two years. I thank all the men that have been in my life for the insight and understanding that I now have. During that time I also came to know someone who was to help me with communication in the media. There were a number of misunderstandings along the way, fortunately. The result has been that I now understand even better that men and women communicate differently. Women learn to communicate through emotions, which are related to the right brain hemisphere's way of communicating. Men use the left brain hemisphere's way of communicating, where emotions are not talked about, but are hidden. This is of course an exaggerated explanation.

However, I do know that the left brain hemisphere represents the masculine part of each person, while the right brain hemisphere represents the feminine. This is true for both women and men. When this is the way men and women communicate, misunderstandings are bound to occur.

*What kind of problems did that pose for you, more exactly?*

A conflict arose in me. I'm a woman, but was taught to refrain from showing my feelings. Perhaps that's why I studied economics, a field that has been dominated by men. Emotions raged within me, but I was hard on the outside. I felt I shouldn't cry or show emotions, for I had learned that meant weakness. The feelings accumulated within me until I really hit the wall. I hadn't learned anything about the way of thinking that I now use, and I had to go through a lot before I understood. When one shares feelings and talks about them, it may sometimes be interpreted as boasting. When one shares genuinely from the heart, not meaning to brag, it hurts a lot when someone says you're bragging. In addition, "feminine hormones," as some men call them, rage away. Emotions, emotions and even more emotions.

*What's the solution?*

I believe that both men and women need to learn about how we function in accordance with what we have within, in order to find balance. Balance is important in everything. Balance in the brain, balance in feelings. We have a lot to learn from each other if we want to.

I've asked many men about why they think that there are fewer men than women at my courses. Some have said that self-development is for old ladies, or "it's something that my wife does." Some say that they think self-development means talking about emotions, and that's not for men.

Tor Arild wrote this to me in an e-mail:

> "ESP is a safe course for men. It's a relief to go to a course where feelings are dealt with on the inside and not the outside. For a man, it can be challenging enough to be at a course with women who are experts at turning every emotional stone in their emotional life in an articulate manner—while the man sits there doing the same himself, but with concepts and notions like a fossil in this area."

If it's normal for men to think like that, then we must communicate an explanation about what self-development is and help men to understand that "From gut feeling to goal-oriented self-development" involves dealing with one's own feelings on the inside and not on the outside. In this respect I feel that we women could use a little more balance. I know that I, in my private life, have been good at getting men to describe their feelings and talk about them again and again. At the courses, on the other hand, I'm the only one talking about emotions and feelings, in order to teach men and women to deal with their own emotions within themselves. It's a relief to be developing and acknowledging. Now I've finally been able to change in that way.

# Assignment for the ninth week

You are to continue using the Nightfilm this week too. If you didn't finish working with goals last week, just continue this week. In addition you will now use the technique for transforming the truths and incidents that you wish to change. You've already made note of something that you wish to change in Exercise 8, and you're ready to work with it this week.

### Exercise 9: The Creative Corner for transformation

- Close your eyes and count down from 7 to 1. Now you only need to take a deep breath at each number. When you've reached number 1, assume that you are in your inner room, and that you are in The Creative Corner.

- **Step 1:** Think about your present situation. Consider carefully whatever might be difficult, or whatever you feel is stopping you. Analyze it, think about it from different angles, and notice whatever feelings you have. Before going on to the next step, take a deep breath and make sure that you feel relaxed.

- **Step 2:** Think that you're about to find the reason for the difficulty or whatever it is you feel is stopping you. Hold an intention that you will arrive at the cause for the situation. Ask the question: What is the cause? or Why did this happen? Then remain quietly in The Creative Corner and silence your mind. Give yourself plenty of time. Perhaps thoughts, ideas, feelings or some memory will come to you. No matter what comes, grip it and consider what it may reveal to you. When you've found something—perhaps a memory, an incident or a feeling, then continue to the next step. In this second step you can also invite parts of yourself, or you may invite someone you would like to communicate with.

- **Step 3**: This is the step for transformation. This will help you to cause the memory, incident or feeling to be replaced with a new truth in your subconscious, thereby creating a different reaction from now on. Think back to a time just before the memory, incident or feeling that you want to transform occurred in your past, and now use your imagination to create it all over again, this time with a positive result for you. Use your imagination, and exaggerate. You are the transformation, and that means that you are to be in it with thoughts and feelings. When the transformation is done, continue to the final step in the process. If there is someone that you need to forgive, whether it be yourself or another, you can do it now, in this step.
- **Step 4**: In this step you are to imagine you are already living your daily life as you wish it to be. You cope well with whatever you encounter, everything is fine and positive, and you enjoy smooth flow.

When you want to end the session, use the procedure for counting out as described in Exercise 1. You may need to do the transformation exercise a number of times before achieving the desired result.

### An example of a transformation

**Step 1:** I'm allergic to sweet peppers. My throat swells and it's quite serious. Every time I'm at a restaurant I must be careful that there are no sweet peppers in the food. I've lived this way for many years.

**Step 2:** My intention is now that I will arrive at the cause for this allergy to sweet peppers. My thoughts wander back to a time when I was very young and we were eating dinner at home in our kitchen. The atmosphere was tense and not very good. I ask myself what this has to do with the allergy? The answer that comes within me is that dinner that night was a casserole with sweet peppers in it.

**Step 3:** I think that I'm entering the kitchen again. This time there's laughter and joy around the dinner table. We eat the casserole with the sweet peppers in it and we immensely enjoy it. To exaggerate, I envision that jokes are being told and the laughter just about raises the roof. We were even allowed to sing at the table. I take those good feelings with me to the fourth step.

**Step 4:** I envision that I'm eating dinner at a restaurant with a friend. The food contains sweet peppers, but I don't notice that until my friend says: "Have you forgotten that you are allergic to sweet peppers?" I'm glowing and happy when I say that I'm healthy now and that I love to eat sweet peppers. We enjoy the dinner, and I'm happy that I now can eat all kinds of foods.

### An example of a dialogue

**Step 1:** I come home from a visit with a friend and I feel very sad. I don't know why, I'm just very down and out.

**Step 2:** I invite the part of myself that feels sad. I have an impression that she's a little girl, and I ask her to sit with me. I ask her why she's sad, and then I silence my mind so that I may notice the answer. I let her tell me all that she feels about her problem.

**Step 3:** We then have a dialog where I use my new insight to help her to be happy. I tell her that she doesn't need to take things personally, because people have different truths. I get her to feel valued and supported. When I'm finished telling the little girl about my insight, I imagine that I'm embracing her and placing her in my heart.

**Step 4:** I'm happy and very content and feel just great. I continue my daily life and all is well. Nothing can disturb my feeling of calmness. I dare to set my boundaries in a good way. It's now safe to say what I mean to others, and I'm happy and proud of myself.

# *Sympathy versus empathy*

*At the courses you talk a lot about the difference between sympathy and empathy. Most people feel that they know what sympathy is, but what do you mean by that?*

If someone is in pain or difficulty, we ask them how they are, and then they start telling about it. Most of us have learned that to be sympathetic we need to be nice people who are willing to listen, and say something like "that's horrible" if the person is suffering. But is that really such a nice thing to do?

Not only do we confirm their misery by repeating how unfortunate they are when someone is in pain or difficulty, but we make sure that we say it several times. We let each other talk extensively about how terrible things are, and in that way we reinforce the feeling of being down, and both of us remain sitting there with a feeling of depression.

*Perhaps this is another syndrome, "soak in dissatisfaction" syndrome?*

Perhaps. But also this comes from an inner truth, and it's important to transform it if we really want to help.

*What about empathy?*

Empathy is the ability to see the whole person. That gives us an understanding that we don't get when we "sympathize" and reinforce another's sadness so that we both get exhausted by the negativity.

*How then should we express that we understand that another person is in a difficult situation and that we would like to help?*

It's better to say: "I see that you're in a difficult situation, and see that it's not easy." Let the other person speak, and give supporting comments. At the same time you can think that you're stepping back and sending some good thoughts their way. That means that while you're standing there, you can radiate some good feelings, which is better than the negativity that's radiated when giving sympathy.

It's important to be aware of the thoughts that I have in my mind. They influence me and my body in addition to influencing what I radiate outward.

Another thing to think about, is that if I go around talking to others about everything that's wrong, then I can cause others to worry unnecessarily.

Your Nightfilm book is a good buddy to give the worries to. You can write down everything that you might have said to others, but that would have been damaging and depressing for them.

Pay attention to your behavior in your daily life. How do you react when someone is experiencing difficulty? Use what I've described above, and you will see and feel a difference.

# Comprehensive
# communication in the whole

"Be the change you want to see in the world"
—Mahatma Gandhi (1869–1948)

*You talk a lot about being a part of a whole, and that this whole includes every living organism on our planet. Do you really mean that we can communicate with all living matter, even when there is no spoken language?*

In order to answer your question I need to first explain what I mean by a whole.

We've already mentioned "the server" that all of us are connected to through a shared network. This "server" contains all knowledge from all that is living, including those who have lived before us. The

Delta brainwave frequencies are the key that gives us access to a mutual connection with "something greater" than ourselves.

Not everyone has a physical language they can use. I've had many course participants who work with people who are not able to express themselves with a physical language, but who nonetheless can communicate using the ESP senses' three ways to perceive information.

*I experience that often with my wife. She can suddenly start talking about something that I'd just been thinking about. It's never seemed particularly magical to me—not after 25 years of marriage.*

That's because this is a form of communication we haven't learned to be aware of, so when we do it deliberately and consciously it's looked upon as mystical or supernatural. It's not mystical or supernatural at all, it's completely natural. It's splendid that we can learn to become aware of this non-physical form of communication again by using our ESP sense.

Animals are another group that don't use a physical language. That doesn't mean that they don't communicate, because they have an ESP sense to communicate with.

*I would call that instinct?*

In humans we call it gut feelings or intuition. Do you remember how the animals in countries that were hit by the tsunami a number of years ago, understood that a catastrophe was on the way? The only animals that died were those that were sick. Think about your dog, Solo. He sits and waits when he knows that your wife is on the way home.

*The most moving story you've told me, Deborah, is about Robin.*

Yes, that's been one of the most powerful experiences I've had. And the core of that story is communication, in every area. It shows us that coincidences are perhaps not by chance at all, but that we can create coincidences and smooth flow in life even when we encounter difficult challenges.

# *Robin's story*

We let Robin's mother, Rita, tell the story:

On March 16, 2010 at 12:15 PM we received a phone call that completely turned our lives upside down, and resulted in giving us a new perspective about life. Not just for me, but for many people around me.

My son Robin, who was 24 years old at the time, had been hit in the head by an avalanche of ice that fell from a seven-story building in Oslo. Shock hit me like lightning and stayed with me for the following weeks. Everything seemed unreal. It almost felt like everything was happening outside of me. But at the same time I was right in the middle of all that was happening. I had no choice.

Seeing it all as if it was outside of me seemed to make it a little easier, so that's how I eventually chose to experience it. I understood very quickly that I needed to have complete focus, almost like an athlete, and this was natural for me because I've trained physically for many years.

Just by chance my present spouse and I had been at one of Deborah's courses in February, and I started using what I had learned there from the very first day. I needed something that could help me to hold focus, maintain balance and keep calm—and I needed to set some goals for myself along the way, especially short-term goals.

I sat down every single day and used the techniques I had learned. Was I happy to have these? You bet! They gave me enormous strength.

There were several "coincidences" that day that saved Robin's life. The right people were present, among others a young boy who had the presence of mind to quickly call for an ambulance, and who also knew how to give first aid. The ambulance was luckily right in the vicinity. Robin was unconscious when it arrived.

Within 20 minutes Robin had been transported to Ullevål University Hospital. They found that Robin had a fractured skull from his forehead to his neck. His lungs were filled with fluid and blood, and head injuries were found. We were finally able to talk to a doctor after several hours. We were then told that Robin had been clinically dead for ten whole minutes. He had been resuscitated, his lungs had been cleared and he was placed in a respirator. We were told that he wouldn't have made it if he hadn't been in such good physical condition.

At that point in time no one knew how this would go, and no one knew in the months that followed either. It was grueling to live with the uncertainty.

The day after the accident, March 17, it was decided to operate and remove part of his skull in order to avoid too much pressure in his head. Some critical days followed. We didn't know if Robin would make it. Our relief was overwhelming when we were told several days later that he was out of the worst danger. My present spouse contacted Deborah on March 18 without my knowledge. She sent a text message to me to tell me that she had already begun working with Robin. It might sound strange to some people, but we could in fact feel that she was present in Robin's hospital room, although she was physically far away. The support from her was priceless.

Many operations followed, due to accumulation of fluids in his head. Complications steadily occurred during the following days, weeks and months. Some more serious than others. Like a roller coaster, sometimes up, sometimes down. After a while the neurologists and surgeons were at a loss. "The case of Robin" was very complicated, and they had never seen anything like this before.

There were many long rounds, greater and lesser decisions to make together with the physicians. There were many messages and meetings where they prepared us for the worst by saying things like "he's not going to make it" or "we need to let nature take it's course," etc.

A solution spontaneously appeared when an infection occurred in his abdomen due to the drain. Doctors had placed a drain from his head down to his abdomen to remove fluids. Due to this infection they decided to remove all drains, since they involved additional risk of infections. Everyone hoped that he would be able to get by without them—and he's done exactly that since then!

Deborah was by now well on her way with Robin, and she was informed about his condition the entire time. So when we were told about the infected drain, we felt that he most likely was not meant to have a drain.

Robin was helped by a respirator, through an opening in his throat, until June. The doctors tried to remove it several times, but he had problems breathing on his own. The first time they took it out, they wanted to put it back in again the next day, but by then the opening in his throat had closed itself ... This was not a coincidence either.

He was in a coma for several months. Everyone waited and waited. The doctors began to be impatient. No motor movement ... no, this isn't good ... There should have been a lot more happening by now. Robin moved a finger just a little bit now and then ... moved an arm a little bit ... but not when asked to.

I knew that Deborah was working in her way, and I did the best I could with the tools I had learned. It felt so good and secure to be in touch with her, and we conferred about how we could work together. This gave me the strength to endure.

The situation was now reversed. Now the doctors were impatient and we were patient. We knew that he was in there. The doctors didn't have much hope that this would go the right way. They were vague. We were positive, we believed in Robin and felt that he just needed time.

When we are asked if we understood how serious the situation was, I must admit that I refused to accept what others assumed. I relied on my gut feeling, that told me something else. That Robin would get better. I've "known" that within myself the whole time, but also that I had to be there.

Deborah never gave up; I'm so proud of her. What strength. She received a lot of messages and phone calls from me when it felt like we were going through the worst storms. She guided me elegantly through them. She gave me courage and strength. She was always calm and steady. Deborah became the one I could lean on, together with what I had learned at her course. I became better at relying on myself and what I in fact could accomplish.

Robin had been at Ullevål University Hospital for five months. At the end of August he was moved to our local hospital in Tønsberg. Even the most optimistic in the medical establishment had lost hope by the time we arrived in Tønsberg. No one says it clearly to you. Hints are dropped. At the same time, he was considered to be a medical miracle, even while he was still at Ullevål.

A quote written by the chief physician at Ullevål on August 31: "It is possible that the patient has shown some progress regarding response with eye movement, but it is very minor and does not give grounds to believe that he will be considerably better even if he survives for a long time."

When we came to Tønsberg Hospital, Deborah came for a physical visit to Robin for the first time. That was on October 18. She said that he was now ready for new strides.

Now things really began to happen. The boy was suddenly in gear. The most unbelievable is that he has regained most everything. Not just motor movement of arms and legs, but also tiny things that the neurologists and we had been waiting for. He uses his fingers, he can press buttons. Very weakly at present, but nonetheless, it seems magical. He does thumbs up when Deborah is going to come. He knows.

He's left all of us incredulous. The doctors couldn't believe their own eyes. What is happening? A conversation with the chief physician in the neurology department at Tønsberg Hospital: "Rita, I must honestly admit that this is the last thing we expected, this is surprising."

Everyone wonders when wonders happen! But they are also very happy for us.

To you, Deborah, words are insufficient, but nonetheless:

Dear, dear Deborah, thank you for traveling with us on this journey. It has definitely been a bumpy ride, but you have stood firm with us, calm and spreading warmth the whole way, no matter what. You have given us so much, Deborah.

Every single day for the first months after the accident I used what you had taught me, with your guidance along the way. Robin *shall* recover. I gave it my all and had full focus.

I quickly found that it gave me large amounts of new energy, drive and after a while even joy, difficult as it is to believe that. When looking back I've wondered how I managed to use those tools so faithfully during the first "time of shock." I just did it, simply by survival instinct I suppose. Through this process I got a greater overview of my life. Here and now. Together with a feeling of inner peace and better contact with myself.

I sent lots of loving thoughts, also to those who were around me. I used the Nightfilm technique, which I've found to be a unique tool. Things fall easily into place.

The past nine months have been very special. An existence at a hospital, every day, several hours a day. With all that's involved of shock, grief, despair, hope and trust. An endless stream of people to relate to. A steady stream of people with new messages, various opinions about one thing and another, repeated statements that Robin would not survive, and uncertainty the whole time. It has been very intense, almost indescribable!

I have chosen to be with Robin every day during these months. I believe that having someone that loves you at your side has healing power.

Robin has only had positive people around him. People who have believed in him with all of their heart. Father, brother, sweetheart and friends have never given up on him. While he was in a coma we assumed the whole time that he heard us and understood what we talked about. He has been surrounded by love and good energy.

I'm writing this because I'm trying to convey an image of what you have contributed. As an invisible helper. One can influence people around one to function in a positive manner, with love and caring. Sometimes one needs help and support from outside.

Many thanks, Deborah, ... we are forever filled with gratitude. You have given us so much of your precious time. You have been a steady rock for me to rely on. You are an earthbound angel! — While Robin is on his way to becoming a medical miracle, in many ways.

I wish you the best of luck with your work for a better fellowship and another way to communicate with each other. You really show that we humans have greater possibilities than we as children were brought up to believe.

A great big warm hug from Rita and the gang (December 4, 2010).

*This is an unbelievably powerful story, Deborah, and it contains some elements that are perhaps completely unexplainable, mystical, even supernatural for many people.*

*Maybe we should try to approach the subject from the down-to-earth perspective that you are so fond of?*

*A doctor once told me about dogs that could predict epileptic seizures in people long before the patient had symptoms. Does something similar happen when one communicates with a person who is in a coma?*

I think that a coma is a state of being in Delta, with connection to "the server" we've talked about. When we have access to Delta, it is possible to communicate with a person who is in a coma, yes. My mission, I feel, is to show people the possibilities they have—through teaching courses and now in book form. We offer guidance in the use of the techniques for course participants, but I don't practice as a therapist of any kind. However, now and then my gut feeling can be so strong that I cannot say no, as in the case of Robin.

*Tell us how you experienced that, Deborah.*

It began when I received an e-mail in March. A participant wrote asking for help: "I ask you, Deborah, if you have the possibility, time and desire to help, please send some positive thoughts to Rita and Robin, they need it so badly now."

I had heard about it on TV the day before, and it's natural for me when I hear about such things to include them in a Nightfilm. So when a course participant wrote to me to ask for help, I couldn't say no. I accepted it within myself, and started as I usually do.

First I defined the goal. If I was to help, the goal must be: *Robin is completely healthy, with new possibilities in life.*

The next step was to break the goal down into tasks and get started.

I still remember the first time I invited Robin into my inner room, because he showed himself to me as an image. I hadn't yet met him physically. He radiated an unbelievable goodness, with lots of good humor. He pointed to his hair and said: "My hair is important for me!" while he was styling and fixing it. I had to smile, because I was surprised that was the first thing that he mentioned. Through that comment, I understood that they had shaved his hair in order to operate. His mother smiled when I told her about the hair comment, and she said: "His hair is important for him, and yes, he has an unbelievably good sense of humor."

I invited him into The Creative Corner every day, talked to him and bolstered him for what was yet to come. He was in shock, so I talked to him about fear and other things that he needed to talk about. It might feel as if one is talking to oneself, but that makes no difference to me. I had a lot of very meaningful conversations "with myself." In addition to the conversations, I envisioned that I sent love, support and the cleansing light that I use in order to strengthen him mentally and physically. I updated his status in a Nightfilm every evening, with new information I had received from within myself as well as conversations and messages from Rita, Robin's mom.

*That sounds like an extensive and time-consuming process.*

Yes, patience is required. I've "talked" a lot to Robin, promising that we'll be patient and do things in his tempo. We also talked about the fear of being present in the body due to pain. He didn't feel pain, but was afraid of doing so.

I guided Rita about how we could use the tools together, and we talked about things that were important for Robin to communicate. For example that we must not talk "over his head", but directly to him. He could both hear and understand, even though speech wasn't displayed.

We also talked about forgiveness, that it doesn't help to focus on blaming anyone, not even in this case. We needed good thoughts full of love in order to reach the goal.

After several months I received a go ahead from Robin. "Now I can take a new step, my body is ready," he said. "By chance" he was transferred to Tønsberg Hospital, quite close to where I live. Talk about solutions for the whole! We could now meet each other physically as well.

I went to the hospital on October 18, entered the room and greeted Robin. It was a powerful meeting, very touching. I started working—counted myself down from seven to one into my inner room, tuned in to the good, healing frequencies that Delta consists of, and thought light and love into his body. I felt that I was to focus on various points. When I was finished, I knew that change would now come.

In the days that followed, I received one message after another from Rita, and when I came to the hospital for the second time, the change was enormous. When I was finished and was about to say good-bye to Robin, he lifted his arm and held my hand tightly. It's difficult for me to talk about it, because after months of work it was such a great moment. A feeling that is impossible to describe.

The improvements were enormous from one visit to the next. He can now turn himself in bed when I need to focus on his back. I've also received photos of Robin where he's practicing on stairs. We're on the way to the goal.

*Along the way, did you ever doubt that it would turn out well?*

Just once, for ten minutes, I did doubt that we would reach the goal. I remember that, in my inner room—The Creative Corner—I brought Robin with me to sit on the sofa. I said rather sternly to him: "Robin, you must hang on, now you need to decide. We've worked so much, so now you need to stay here. I'll help you, but you must not leave now." I was really upset, for I understood that it was not I who doubted. He looked at me and said: "Come on, what are you waiting for?" From that day I've known that we would reach the goal.

Robin and I have set many goals now, and the last time I was with him before finishing off this book, we agreed that we would go to the cinema to see a really good movie when he's ready. Rita smiled and said that he loves to watch movies, so that's a good goal. I'm looking forward to that day, and see myself sitting in the cinema with Robin. The boy with the radiant eyes, styled hair, and fantastic warmth and humor, who has taken my heart by storm. This has been worth every single day that I've worked on my own life, towards a goal that enables me to give to others.

## Sunday, February 27, 2011

I'm visiting Robin. Together with me are Robin, Rita, Øyvind (Rita's present spouse, who was the one who contacted me almost a year ago), Robin's brother Thomas, and Robin's girlfriend. We decided to write a short, updated status report for this book before I left.

Rita and Thomas told that they received a rather shocking surprise during the weekend two weeks earlier. "Mom was in Robin's room and I went there and stood in the doorway," Thomas told us. Suddenly Robin said: "Thomas, come here." It was unbelievable, intense, even when we'd been waiting for this to happen. It feels great, and we're looking forward to what the future will bring. Thomas also told us that what happened has made possible a different view about life's values and the importance of appreciating what is here and now.

"We have Robin back," Rita said. "He's talking, also in whole sentences. His balance is much better and he can walk with some help, and he's on his way to doing it on his own."

We all agree that everything is possible. When I get up to go, Robin smiles and says: "Bye Deborah," exactly as I have envisioned so many times in The Creative Corner.

# Assignment for the tenth week

We've now come to the last exercise in the book. In addition to your Nightfilm, your assignment this time is using The Creative Corner with your eyes open. I recommend that you do the basic exercise for relaxation once a day this week as well.

**Exercise 10: The Creative Corner with eyes open**
- Find a comfortable position and close your eyes.
- Take a deep breath, and feel your body relax from your head to your toes. Don't think of the numbers this time, just relax. Think that you tune in to the feeling of being in your inner room.
- When you have that feeling, open your eyes. Take another deep breath and register that same feeling.
- Practice doing this until you can easily get the feeling of being in your inner room with your eyes open.
- When you've accomplished this while sitting, the time has come for you to tune in to that feeling while standing, with your eyes open.

You are now ready to do this at any time during your day when you need to concentrate, make decisions or when you come across something difficult. This will help you to remain calm in any situation.

# Deborah on TV

*You would like to remove the mysticism associated with using ESP, Deborah.*
*Why then did you choose to participate in the TV series "Sensing Murder,"*
*that most people associate with supernatural phenomena and clairvoyance?*

I remember reading in a newspaper that a TV series was to be
produced where "clairvoyants" would be working on unsolved murder
cases to see if they could find new evidence or solutions. My first thought
was "No, that's not right for me, since I'm working to teach people that
the ESP sense is something quite natural that everyone can use to create
a better life." I remember feeling indignant. Using gut feelings was very
natural for me, but on TV they would make it appear to be something
supernatural. Remember, up until that time I had used my abilities to
regain my health and create a better life. What happened then, was that
I wrote about it in a Nightfilm. Among other things, I wrote that if this
was to be, that it would be a series that took the matter seriously. After
three weeks I was contacted by *Nordisk Film*.

*Yes, you were recommended by several people we had asked when we were casting.*

Then I wrote a new Nightfilm and entered The Creative Corner, where I had a conversation with myself. I had work and a family to consider, and I knew that it would be a hotly debated TV series. I finally decided to meet with them to see what they were thinking of.

At that first meeting I was shown into a room where I was to sit in front of a camera, hold an envelope and tell what information I could get from it using my ESP sense. I didn't have the slightest idea of what to expect, so I thought that I would just say whatever I felt.

Since I am a kinesthetic person, I still remember the feeling I had while sitting with that envelope. I felt that my body was more and more on fire, so I finally said that it felt like I was on fire. They were somewhat incredulous, since the person whose picture was in the envelope had died in a fire. I must admit that I was rather perplexed myself. Afterwards I decided to participate in the series in order to show that everyone has gut feelings that can be trained. One of my goals was set there and then: "I will train the police to develop stronger gut feelings."

*How are you doing with that goal?*

We've had many participants who work in the police force at our course. Who knows? When they read this book and find out that it isn't so mystical, perhaps even more officers will attend the course, creating a very strong police force. I have a humorous vision in my mind that I sometimes share with others. Just think of a billboard with a picture of a police officer standing at a border crossing to Norway with text that says "Don't come here for criminal purposes, for we can read you like an open book!"

It's important to be able to laugh at oneself and not—as I did earlier—at everyone else.

The main reason why I agreed to participate in "Sensing Murder" was my intention to show people that they can train themselves to have stronger gut feelings, and that this is something natural. I am in addition a person who wants to help, so if my participation could help someone, that would be fantastic.

*What was it like to work with cases in "Sensing Murder," compared to things you had done previously?*

This was something completely different from what I had done earlier. I had mostly explored how I could use my ESP sense to help myself, to help others, to find objects, to see how an object could tell a story, to find leaks in a house, to find problems in cars, and so on. "Sensing Murder" was a very intense experience for me.

*I remember many horrible cases in "Sensing Murder." How did you cope with that?*

Since I experienced the tragedies and suffering of others, I had to cope with my own feelings as well as remain humble and understanding of everyone involved. I had to have a perspective that helped me to see the whole situation. It was difficult. At the same time, the camera was always there, focused on me in order to record the overpowering moments. This led to pressure about what was expected of me, that I also had to cope with. There was a lot happening all at once, and it was completely different from what I expected when I agreed to participate.

*Do you remember any special cases?*

All of the cases were special, each in their own way. In one episode it felt like I had been shot in the head. I really had to work to transform that. The images and experiences were so overpowering that I had to work for several weeks to get rid of them.

Another difficult case was the one where a woman had been found in a freezer. I remember that I had led them to the house where it had happened, and stood outside to find more information. I thought of a very small room, but I had to ask myself: "What little room?"

Then I suddenly became ice cold; it felt like I had ice all over my body, although it was warm outside. I didn't know if I dared to tell what I felt, for I thought that sort of thing only happened in horror movies;

that a dead body is found in a freezer. I also remember asking myself if she had been alive when she was put in there, and I was led to feeling my own pulse, something that told me that she was still alive at that point.

Another extremely unpleasant experience was on the border between Norway and Sweden. We were taking a break, so the cameras were turned off. Suddenly I smelled a bonfire which made me remember grilling hot dogs and marshmallows on a bonfire with my children in the woods. The smell was so intense that I asked the others if they could smell it, but they only looked at me strangely. When the cameras were on again, I suddenly understood that I had perceived information kinesthetically. The victim in the case had been burned in a bonfire.

I also remember having a strong reaction in Denmark, when I stood on exactly the cobblestoned place where the victim had been found. One gets somewhat startled at a time like that.

It was important for me to help people and not to frighten anyone. I know that when I receive information kinesthetically, through bodily sensations, it's important that I don't dramatize or do things vehemently. I had to remember to retain control and remain in balance, so that the family members and TV audience would not experience it as brutal.

*You also participated in "The Power of Spirits." What was that like?*

I wasn't completely comfortable with that show. I don't believe in "the power of spirits." In my opinion, spirits do not have power. The producer, however, said that if I really wanted to demystify these things, then it was important for me to participate. After a Nightfilm, I decided that he was right, and I chose to participate.

My belief that humans influence negatively due to fear and imagination was confirmed. Just think about how children react to ghost stories. This fear is stored in our iceberg.

The spirits do not have power, but because we go around with this stored fear, we give power not to the spirits, but to the fear. We become paralyzed and overwhelmed.

The spirits are also a part of "the server," and we can receive information from them that may be used to help. Under traumatic circumstances, the transition from the physical dimension to the non-physical can be difficult, but I feel that we don't need to dramatize it. When we don't understand how we receive information, fear and imagination are allowed to take over. We can see visions and hear auditory "sounds," but it is nonetheless information that is received by the ESP sense.

I don't believe there are so many vagrants in the spiritual world. In fact, I believe that the spirits have been given a bad reputation that they don't deserve. We need to stop blaming spirits. It's our own fear that causes discomfort for us.

*There were many special stories in that series. Are there any that you remember especially well?*

Yes, the episode when I was at an island called Karmø where there were a lot of disturbances in a house, such as objects moving or falling for no apparent reason. The man who lived there easily picked up impressions of energy with his ESP sense because he had previously experienced something traumatic, which can make people become more open and receptive. If we don't understand the information that comes to us through our ESP sense, then a negative flow may be started. He felt that the disturbances in the house were rather thrilling, and the Law of Attraction says that we get more of what we focus on. After I had been there it was quiet for a while, but I later heard that more disturbances had occurred. This was most likely due to the attention he gave to the matter and the excitement he felt, which resulted in more disturbances. What we focus upon, and thereby attract, is a choice that each one of us can make. However, explaining such phenomena is not within the subject matter in this book, and will be explained in more detail in our next book.

I also remember another episode that gave me much food for thought afterwards. I walked around in a house and inspected as

I usually do. I sat on the bed in one of the rooms and entered The Creative Corner. I suddenly felt a tightening in my chest, and since I know that I receive information kinesthetically, I asked myself what the feeling was telling me.

Then I perceived an image in my mind's eye of a young boy who told me that it was his bed and that he had asthma. I could have let fear and imagination run wild, as I had physically become very short of breath. When my answer came to me the tightness disappeared and I could tell what I had learned. It was true. The boy who slept in this room did have asthma. This is about understanding oneself and how we function as humans. I participated in that TV series for two seasons, and I understand that when I demystify and explain those things in my way, then it isn't particularly exciting or entertaining TV when they are trying to produce mystical and supernatural phenomena.

*Since then other shows have appeared on TV that are even more extreme. Would you consider participating in anything like that?*

Do I really need to answer that? I think the readers understand that the answer is no. I don't like it when the ESP sense is used to produce frightening TV shows. What one chooses to believe in is important. If I believe in evil, then I attract more evil.

I made a choice many years ago due to an inner experience. I found in my iceberg that I had learned about heaven and hell, and if I was bad then I would go to hell. That was a truth that I had to transform. Today I choose to believe that heaven is a symbol for something good, and that the world we live in can be hellish if we focus on all that is negative. That is what I experienced in my own life.

*What have your TV experiences taught you?*

As a mentor and consultant in "Britain's Psychic Challenge" I saw the importance of understanding oneself. The "alternative" was portrayed as a vague, floating world that people escape to when they cannot cope with life. That's a mistake. One talks about love one minute and in the next a warlike competition is created. I saw how some people elevated themselves and cultivated the ego—for example the man who claimed to be a healer on the same level as Jesus. You remember him, Kim?

*Yes, he was peculiar! I remember that he said "many people tell me I remind them of Jesus Christ."*

It's tragic if people really believe that. When I told him that, he said OK, but you need me to make good TV. I don't believe that good TV should be like that, and I rejected him.

*The basic idea behind "Psychic Challenge" was a neutral starting point. We wanted to test those who said they were clairvoyant. The TV series has been a success throughout the world, having been aired in 19 countries. What do you believe is the reason that so many people are interested in these phenomena?*

I've thought a lot about what makes us seek out the mystical. As I see it, the reason is that we lack a magical daily life. Some have said to me that I shouldn't remove the mystique, but I believe that we should rather find out what it is that the mystical is replacing in our lives. We're tired of stress and rushing around and are looking for inner peace, but we can end up following a path that leads to imbalance.

My life wasn't the same after I appeared on TV. When I was out shopping people would come up to me just to touch me, saying that they'd seen me on TV. People phoned at all hours. One man called and said that I had to help him or he would commit suicide. Others phoned to ask me to find objects, and others wanted know what was in store for them in the future. I'd been portrayed as mystical and special, one who had the answer to everything. Me(!), who had only wanted to show that everyone has gut feelings that can be used to create a good life. An ordinary woman with well-trained gut feelings, and no mysticism.

*I know that it's important for you to communicate that people must create their own future and make their own choices. What do you think when you see all those who use their so-called clairvoyance to help others with financial matters or difficult love affairs?*

Let's put it this way, Kim: I'm very concerned about this. I don't think it's wise for me to say too much here, for the book would become too long, but I'll give you an example.

My mother once went to a fortune teller and was told that she would travel over a large ocean and have three children before returning to Norway. The fortune teller ended the séance by saying that my mother would die when she was 72 years old. Since the first part came true, my mother began to believe the last part as well. For many years she thought about and talked about dying when she was 72.

So the natural thing happened, and it became a self-fulfilling prophecy. Things that we have feared and thought about enough times finally become real, as truths in the iceberg. When she was 72, my mother was diagnosed with breast cancer. Then we, her children, intervened. I told her that she needed to decide that what the fortune teller had predicted was not going to come true. I talked to her a lot in my inner room and used the Nightfilm technique to update her. She is still alive and well at age 81. We are all able to influence others in a positive manner, fortunately.

People who make such predictions steer the lives of others and take from them their own choices and possibilities. I know that some of them have attached their name to mine and have said that they've been to my course, so now they can tell fortunes. In that case they have not paid attention in class, for I—to the contrary—would like to prohibit that kind of fortune telling.

*You don't approve of expensive telephone services where people claim that they can predict the future?*

Many years ago I wanted to look into fortune telling, so I said yes to spending a day or two at a fortune-telling café. I was to give guidance by holding an object, while others used tarot cards and other helpful materials. It was a tragic experience. People sat there who had great problems in their own lives, and when no customers were around they asked each other for help. One of them smelled strongly of alcohol. For me, this is a way of abusing other people.

It's scary to hear that even politicians who are responsible for our government, cannot in fact steer their own lives, but use fortune tellers. My advice is to learn techniques that make it possible for you to make your own choices and pay attention to your own gut feelings. You may start by using this book—it costs less than several minutes of those fortune-telling telephone services. In addition you can create whatever you like.

*Despite mixed feelings about your experiences with TV, Deborah, will we see you on the screen again?*

TV is a fantastic platform for reaching out to many people. That's just what I want, to get as many people as possible to understand that they can take control of and be responsible for their own lives. So if the right concept turns up, you might be seeing me on TV again.

# Continuing your journey

"Life may only be understood backwards, but must be lived forwards"
—Søren Kirkegaard (1813–1855)

*We're approaching the end of the book, Deborah, and now the readers will take what they have read with them on their journey through life. What is your most important tip to them?*

If you would like to make changes, I recommend starting with the chapter "How to use this book." Following the instructions that we recommend takes a few weeks, but you'll notice results very quickly. Things will happen along the way. In addition, change has already started to take place if you've already read this book.

*You've shared so much in this book, so perhaps you can tell about how you practice all of this?*

I write a Nightfilm every evening. That enables me to go to sleep without worries, and have a deep, good sleep that's so important for good health. That also prepares for the next day. I *live* every moment. If I encounter something that I don't like or that is negative for me emotionally, I enter The Creative Corner and transform it. In addition, I have a vision that I stretch towards every day. If I get new ideas, I work with my goal journal.

I remember to remind myself that I am a human who has enormous possibilities, but no one is 100 percent. If I can accomplish 80–90 percent of what I set out to do, I'm happy about that. One needs to focus on the percentage that *is* possible to do something about. That creates magical moments.

*That sounds very simple—almost too simple.*

I usually say that the simplest is often the best. Don't complicate anything that in fact is simple—and magical.

*What do you feel is the most important single effect from following the advice in this book, or taking your course?*

Stress disappears, and that opens us for the rest of the possibilities. For example, a calm, harmonious life without worries is achievable.

In addition, the most important understanding that I communicate in this book is that you create your own life, that you sit at the helm and decide the direction of the ship.

The book is not the same as taking the course. I cannot give you the deep training or strengthen your ESP sense, as we do at a course. However, the book will give you insight and tools that will get you on your way to a magical daily life.

*One last question, Deborah. More than 20,000 people have participated in courses with you throughout the years. Are there any stories that you remember particularly well?*

You know, Kim, there are many stories that I bow my head for. When people use my insight to make changes in their own lives, it's always a powerful experience, no matter what the story. There are some people who've been on the verge of suicide due to abuse and a tough life, for example, who tell me of a new life of happiness and harmony. Then I know that every time I share my insight, it means something for others.

I regularly receive thank-you letters from people who feel that I've talked directly to them throughout the whole course, even when there were 140 people there. That's thrilling for me.

Or people who come back to repeat the course who say: "Deborah, I didn't like you the first time I was at your course, but now I understand that it wasn't you. It was all about me." In cases like that I'm glad that I don't take things personally, because I know that it is the reactions of others. It makes me happy that they are able to see it themselves, because that means they are developing themselves and will have a better life.

I also recall a lady in her 80's. She probably doesn't like that I mention her age, so I hope she'll forgive me if she recognizes herself in this story. This woman has participated in many of our courses that take place where she lives, and she's made great changes in her life each time. She is grateful and happy that people never get too old to learn something new. She also likes to come to the free lectures, to get a good hug and give support to my work. She was still working full time the last time I saw her. What a great role model!

There are also some course participants with very disabling handicaps that radiate gratitude because their lives have become easier. No matter who we are or where we are, it's about developing ourselves in a deliberate and conscious manner.

I like Obama's expression: "Yes, we can!" Because we really can!

# Examples from course participants

## Examples for using the Nightfilm technique

### *Marianne*

I have a daughter who's been terribly afraid of getting her driver's license. Every time someone asked if she would be taking driving lessons soon, it led to anger and frustration. She'd say: "Maybe in the Spring," or "There's always someone who can pick me up or drive me." One weekend when she was visiting me we talked about that fear, and she told me why she was afraid. I used a Nightfilm in the following way:

**The Day Today**: Madeleine told me that she is afraid of getting in a car with a stranger, she's afraid to drive in traffic, and afraid of stalling the motor with cars behind her. The prospect of driving in winter is especially scary. Taking the theoretical test also terrifies her. She thinks: How can she manage to pass when so many fail?

**The Day Tomorrow**: Madeleine calls me and I almost can't understand what she says because she is so overcome by happiness. Mom, I've passed the theoretical test and have my driver's license. I love driving, and I'll be driving over to see you soon.

I called her on Monday afternoon and she didn't have time to talk to me because she was busy buying a car. "Yes, and I'll be having my first driving lesson on Wednesday," she said.

It also needs to be said that the driving instructor and Madeleine got along very well; she felt secure and looked forward to every lesson. She passed the theoretical test on her first try. She bought a car in January and got her driver's license in April.

## *Kari*

I participated at a course in June this year, and hadn't ever practiced using a Nightfilm earlier. This was new to me, and I was open for using it but had some problems getting started. After a while I got started and had some minor results.

However, the following was a real WOW result:

My son is a Masters student in chemistry, and this involves a lot of lab work. He started in January 2010. During the winter he first became a little sick, and later so sick that it was affecting his studies. He went to a doctor several times without finding out what was wrong or what could be done to help him get better. He had headaches, sore throat, stuffed up nose and little energy. He lagged in his studies and was behind when summer arrived and the lab closed. He was fine during the summer of 2010 and counted on making up for lost time in the fall semester.

He applied for a student loan for the school year 2010/2011, but was turned down because he hadn't kept up with his studies. He appealed the denial and presented statements from his doctor. That's when Mom thought that he needed some help in order to win the appeal.

Examples of Nightfilms I have written:

**The Day Today**: My son would like to finish his education, but cannot do that without a student loan. Waiting for a decision.

**The Day Tomorrow**: He's standing with a letter about the loan in his hand. In the letter it's clearly spelled out that his appeal—and his loan—have been approved. He eagerly turns to his books and starts studying again, and starts the lab work as well.

**Result**: It took some time, but the loan was approved so that he was able to work full time on his studies.

When the semester started, his symptoms came back as well, as in the previous semester. He remained at home in bed and missed a lot of school. His doctor was still unable to help him find out what was the matter, so Mom used her tools again:

**The Day Today**: P is sick, at home in bed without enough strength to go to school or do lab work.

**The Day Tomorrow**: He's with his doctor, and his doctor tells him that he's found the reason for his symptoms. I envision P standing with a report of his exam grades in his hand.

**Result**: Two days later my son called and was, if not so happy, at least relieved that the reason for his symptoms had been found. His guidance counselor had "coincidentally" told him that he had a student a few years ago who had been so allergic to acetone that he had to stop doing lab work. (Acetone is used for cleaning in the lab). It so happens that my son has always had allergies, both food allergies and pollen allergy, so it is possible that he is allergic to even more. He immediately asked his doctor if he could be allergic to acetone. It turned out that he was!

Finding this out was a relief, but a chemistry student who couldn't work in the lab? He quickly realized that he needed to talk to his guidance counselor about how he could finish his studies.

Again, Mom felt that he needed help:

**The Day Today**: P is halfway finished with his studies. He's sitting with the guidance counselor, asking how he can finish his studies.

**The Day Tomorrow**: P is finished with his Master's degree. He's standing with a report of his exam grades in his hand, smiling and very happy.

**Result**: The next day my son called again, and this time he's really pleased!

His guidance counselor had been very understanding and presented several suggestions for alternative assignments that didn't involve lab work. This means that he would be given an adapted study assignment, but earns the same degree that he would if he had finished the ordinary studies. He's just begun the specially adapted studies and hasn't had any exams yet, but now we trust that this will go well! Isn't that great?

## *Pernille*

I'd like to share a Nightfilm with you where one of my goals was included, and this goal has to do with my financial challenges.

**The Day Today**: I've slept well and woke up with a contented boy (my son). We enjoyed our time at the breakfast table, I radiate positive energy that also affects my family, and it feels good to be together. We've been to a puppet show and really enjoyed that. Then I received a bill for a payment towards my student loan in the amount of $1900. I need to phone about that on Monday, because I can't afford to pay it. This makes me feel scared and anxious. I really hope that this situation can be resolved, that I talk to a person who is easy to talk to, and that I'm able to be humble and not afraid. I will work on this in The Creative Corner tomorrow and call in an expert in the field.

**The Day Tomorrow**: Awaken very rested and in good spirits, and this mood spreads to everyone I'm in contact with. I enjoy a quiet morning and drive my son to preschool. I relax and calm myself, get a good overview of the situation before I phone the person who sent the letter about my student loan debt. I feel secure, calm and respectful. I'm able to make this payment. Everything falls into place for all parties and to the best for all. Many thanks

I worked in The Creative Corner and my expert advised me to find all the relevant papers and review my situation.

**Result**: I phoned about the study debt, enjoyed smooth flow and had a pleasant conversation with a nice person. Everything worked out fantastically well.

I'm an educational leader at a school for multi-handicapped students. I've worked a lot with the challenge of being a leader for some people who are older than myself. I always include in my Nightfilms that I radiate positive energy, attract all that is good and enjoy smooth flow, and I've noticed that this is a great help to feel secure and calm.

I enjoy fantastic flow at work and have good relations with the multi-handicapped students. I know that this is because I communicate with my ESP sense.

When I look back in my Nightfilm book, I see that what I have written, has in fact happened.


## Siren

The Nightfilm technique is very effective. This summer we were to visit the zoo and amusement park near Kristiansand and had bought 3-day tickets for various activities. I met people who said that wasn't a good idea, that we would need to stand in long lines since it was the busy season, that we wouldn't be able to find a parking space and that we wouldn't be able to see everything. I used the Nightfilm technique on our trip. We found a parking space and came right on time to all guided tours, and we were able to see and experience all the activities that we had decided on. We didn't stand in any lines and we had a fantastic time. Smooth flow for the whole trip.

I've also helped my parents find smooth flow. They were planning to renovate their bathroom at a time when it was hopeless to get the necessary tradesmen to come. They had been told that they would need to wait for a year. So they decided to do the job themselves, and they became more and more tired because this was a big job. I used the Nightfilm technique. It took only 48 hours for them to get in touch with good workers to do the job.

When I was going to start studying, I needed to find daycare for my daughter. All deadlines for applications to preschools had passed. I decided to apply anyway. I used a Nightfilm and The Creative Corner. After one month my daughter was accepted at preschool.

I'm the board chairman for a condominium owners' association. One day I had a strong gut feeling that some jobs being done for our association were not being done well. When we checked on this, it turned out to be true.

I had a lot of trouble sleeping before I started my self-development. I only slept a few hours each night. I wasn't able to do anything before 10:00 AM. Now I sleep very well and I'm in full swing by 7:00 AM. This result happened very quickly after I started self-development.

When I bought my condominium apartment I had to fix up the bathroom. I didn't know where I'd find the money, so I wrote a Nightfilm about that. I couldn't borrow any more money where I had my mortgage. Then my bank called and suggested that I might want to consolidate all my loans in one bank, so I went there to talk to them. She asked if I needed to borrow more, and I said that I needed to renovate the bathroom, but just the work itself would cost about $32,000. She offered me a loan for $40,000. This bank has always said no when I've asked for help earlier, so this was a strange experience.

A short while ago there were many different workers that were to do various jobs at the condominiums where I live. I included this in my Nightfilm the day before. After driving my little one to school the next day, I arrived home "coincidentally" just as the elevator serviceman came to check the elevators. He didn't have a key with him, and needed help to get into the building. I was in the right place at the right time, and I was even able to participate in checking the elevator. It was a little scary to stand on top of the elevator in the elevator shaft, but was fun too.

Many times I've experienced being in the right place at the right time, with things happening in the correct order, but these are just some examples.

## *Hege*

I write down all that the day has given me, both good and bad. If my day has been demanding, if there have been incidents that hurt me in some way, or negative feelings that have been aroused in me, I write to let them go, completely uncensored. When going through the film afterwards, by watching it without feeling, only watching the actions, I come to a state of peacefulness. The negative and painful feelings are gone. I put them aside. I can still examine and work with them later. This is an enormous difference from how my life was earlier. I was previously stuck in the difficulties for a long time, sometimes for weeks. My thoughts kept spinning, I just couldn't let go and free myself from them. The thoughts won every time. Now I have a tool—in the form of the Nightfilm technique—that allows me to work through them and set them aside the same day that they've happened. It's so unbelievably good to set aside painful or negative incidents. My life is NOW, and it's so good to be able to say that and truthfully mean it. I've been freed from living in the past, as well as from fear that tomorrow will bring the same kind of pain. I live like this more and more in my daily life too, independently from the Nightfilm. I experience things, feelings arise, and then I center myself, count myself down and find peace in my inner room. Then I can return, and I've set aside the incident that shook me up in some way. I then included it in my Nightfilm in the evening.

The Nightfilm technique has made me more aware of my own power to create the contents of my own truths.

I've always been tired and unwell in the mornings. My alarm clock was set to ring an hour before I really needed to get up, because I needed time to wake up. The clock rang again every nine minutes. I slept again between each ring of the clock, and became even more tired and unwell. The first hour of my day was a struggle to groom myself and get off to work. When I arrived at work I was finally "on," and got going because I have a strong will and I'm conscientious about my work. I had an established truth that I was very tired and slow to get going in the morning, and that's the way it was!

All of my Nightfilms about The Day Tomorrow start with: "I awaken healthy, rested and full of energy, happy about all the good that I know this day will bring to me." The result is that I awaken more rested in the mornings. I have more energy and get out of bed without the hour-long slumbering before I get started, as I did earlier. I am in fact ready to meet the day and whatever it brings. I had to experience this for myself in order to believe it. There have been a few days where I didn't write a Nightfilm for various practical reasons, and then I've fallen back into the same old rut.

I use the Nightfilm especially in connection with my daily work as a team leader. This is a very demanding job with many daily duties, much to take into consideration, colleagues to follow up, meetings where routines for solving assignments are worked out, etc. Resources are scarce and I feel I'm being stretched in several different directions in order to achieve goals and results. I'm basically a positive and solution-oriented person, and have always worked towards goals. However, this autumn has been especially demanding. I've managed to avoid becoming stressed, something I wouldn't have managed if I hadn't worked consciously with myself and used what I've learned at Deborah's course.

In the Nightfilm about The Day Tomorrow, I write all that is to happen like meetings, follow-ups, coordination, results, and so on. I write specifically about what I want to achieve, the result I want for assignments, what I'm looking to learn, and that there is dialogue as well as that things happen constructively. In nine of ten instances I experience that things fall into place just as I had prepared in the Nightfilm, first by writing about them and then living them. It feels so good to live the Nightfilm about The Day Tomorrow. I always get these wonderful feelings: delight, humbleness and happiness about results achieved, both my own and those of others as well as the results I accomplish together with others. The pleasure is therefore doubled when the results turn out to be as I had lived them in the Nightfilm. I wish for as many people as possible to experience this force.

In the Nightfilm I honestly and sincerely focus on the positive that I want to achieve or experience. It can be anything, from what some would call trivial daily matters, to greater tasks and goals that demand more of me in a different way. I'm very specific about what I want and what I'm working with, and I'm very careful about the language I choose. It's important to me to find something positive, also in matters which I've experienced as difficult. Every cloud has a silver lining.

I use between ten minutes to half an hour to write the Nightfilm about The Day Today and The Day Tomorrow. I don't know how much time I use on the meditation, because I do that in bed, falling asleep as soon as I've finished The Day Tomorrow.


## *Bodil*

My experiences after using Nightfilms are truly unbelievable. Talk about creating magic in daily life. The one I mention here is just one of many, for I feel that the Nightfilm works all the time, as long as one uses it.

I started writing in my Nightfilm book on April 24, 2010.

On April 29 I was to travel to Iceland with a woman friend. We had also been on a trip together to Madeira in February, and we ended up in the midst of a flood that took many lives.

My friend's daughter became very worried when she saw pictures from the flood on the news, since she knew that her Mom was in the middle of the catastrophe. Things usually turn out well after all, and they did that time too, to make a long story short.

So we were going to Iceland together in April. We had ordered the tickets many months earlier, long before the volcano erupted. When our departure date came closer, she cancelled due to fear of another volcanic eruption (something that didn't stop me).

Suddenly I was to travel to Iceland alone, and that's where the Nightfilm comes in.

I'm sitting with my book in front of me now, while writing this and I see that on April 28, for The Day Tomorrow, I've written that I meet someone on the plane that knows something about nursing. Why nursing, you're certainly thinking. Well, after 17 years I've finally found out what I want to do. In the fall of 2009 it hit me like lightning from a clear blue sky that I was to become a nurse. I got hold of a lot of books about anatomy and began preparing myself to become a student, a year in advance.

After I did the Nightfilm I went to sleep completely calm and convinced that my trip to Iceland would be OK and that I would meet some interesting people this weekend. I had no idea that the Nightfilm would work as well as it did.

I got up and went to my local airport at about 5:00 AM, changing planes in Oslo on the way to Reykjavik. On that flight I sat next to a woman and we quickly started a conversation. It turned out that there were 16 people from the University Hospital in Tromsø on their way to Iceland on that flight. Their plan had been to leave a day earlier, but they'd been delayed a day in Oslo due to the volcanic eruption.

One of those 16 people had turned around in Oslo and returned to Tromsø because he had an important meeting on Monday, and he was afraid that the return flight on Sunday might be cancelled. There was therefore one available spot. This group of nurses had booked everything that they planned to do that weekend, and they invited me to come along for all of it. We started out by being picked up by a bus that took us to the Blue Lagoon, where a table was set and waiting. We had a nice lunch, followed by a lazy swim in the warm lagoon. They invited me to come with them for their whole program the following day, and the whole weekend went like that. On Sunday we went to the airport. The flight took off as planned, and the captain informed us that we had the volcano almost under us on the right hand side. I remember that I wondered if it really was the volcano I had seen, since it looked like there was so much ash. On the news they had said that the volcano had calmed down. When we arrived in Norway we heard that the airport at Reykjavik had been closed again due to new volcanic activity. It was quite clear that there were strong forces that wanted me in Iceland that weekend to meet those people.

The fact that I wrote Nightfilms about being accepted as a nursing student, and that I read the required literature for a year before starting up, must have sent out the right signals. I was accepted at two universities, one at Agder in southern Norway and one in Copenhagen, Denmark. I chose the one called UIA in southern Norway, at their branch in the town of Grimstad. I contacted the woman I had met on the flight to Iceland, as she was the one I had most contact with while I was there. She was naturally interested to hear whether I had been accepted as a student, and I was happy to tell her that I had. Not long after that I received a text message from her that she would be moving from Tromsø with her husband and children, because she had received a three-year PhD scholarship at UIA's branch in Grimstad. Is it possible? We've come to know each other better, she's helped me by giving me valuable advice, and we've also enjoyed our friendship. We're both very happy that we met on that flight, and will be able to enjoy each other's company for at least the next three years.

## Examples for using a goal journal

### Hege H.

I'm sharing a little from my goal journal.

**Goal: I will write books**

What is necessary for me to reach this goal? Secondary-goals that are concrete and goal-oriented are needed. I worked with this goal after my first course at the end of August, and secondary-goals quickly appeared for me, in different ways. Information came to me in ways that make me laugh when looking back. I took it seriously and acted accordingly. I quite literally stumbled across information about a writing school with various modules and opportunities for manuscript follow-up along the way, together with an announcement about a writing competition through my daily work. In all the six years I've worked in this department, I've never seen an internal e-mail about a writing competition before. An invitation from the writing school followed, to become part of a group where writing competitions are regularly made available. I found this last offer in my e-mail in the afternoon, after having thought the very same morning that I would like to try my hand at more writing competitions.

In September, this fall, I completed the first module of a writing course, resulting in my very first short story. A short story I'm proud of for several reasons, but particularly because it satisfied all requirements as to form for a short story.

In November I participated in a writing competition through a trade journal called Welfare. I chose, warily, to try my hand at a second short story this fall. The result of this writing competition was just unbelievably thrilling and enjoyable. I made it to the finals. Not among the top three, but the short story was good enough that they wanted to publish it, and that will happen during 2011.

I started on the next module of the writing course on January 18, 2011.

I have gathered information about all of the publishing houses in Norway, writing competitions and possible paths for those who have concrete manuscript ideas. I checked out the possibilities that exist. I have, through the writing course, established contacts for manuscript follow-up and guidance while writing the text.

So many times I've "lived" that I've reached this goal, some day on the path ahead. I'm patient and work towards my goal without rushing. When I wonder about the quality of what I'm doing, or have other questions, I take them with me to The Creative Corner and get answers from within me and from dialogue with others I've invited to my inner room.

**Goal: To love myself unconditionally**

I've lived alone with my son for ten years. A desire for love and a close relationship to another person has been with me the whole time. My truths that I have come to this world to be lonely, to exist only to help others, to live as a person that no one wants to hold, not even give a compliment to, has overruled this desire in myself for all these years. Until I learned that no change will happen until I transform these truths that lie branded within me.

What is necessary in order to reach this goal? I need to find love of myself, within myself. I must recognize my own worth as the unique person I am, even when naked and without all of the things I do for others every day. I need to live for myself, not for all others. Finally, I want to live happily with myself as well as the rest of the world, without negatively affecting me or others. I want to live in harmony and balance with myself. The day that I can look at myself in the mirror and honestly say "I love you!" is the day I'll be ready to attract a life partner that I'll be able to live happily with. I've managed that this autumn, between the two courses I've been to. I'm able to look at myself in the mirror and honestly say that I'm fond of myself, as I am fond of others around me. That was a very special experience.

I set my own limits in a good way, so that others understand why, and without creating anything negative for myself or others. I've stopped feeling that I'm obliged to give something in return. What I do for others now is done from a genuine wish to make others happy.

I do loving things for myself. I practice every day doing for myself what I've always done for others. This training is quite demanding, but with knowledge about transforming I've come a long way this autumn, something that shows in my entire existence. I'm exiting a shell that I'd built around myself from a very young age, and I'm doing this with feelings of apprehensive thrill and happiness that I cannot describe with words.

## Examples for using The Creative Corner for transformation

### Hege H.

I always ask, when I've experienced something painful or that has created negative emotions in me: Why did this come to me? What am I to learn from this? What have I done to be thwarted in this way? Why has this come back to me again? What have I overlooked, or failed to do something about?

Sometimes the answer comes to me so quickly that I wonder if it's the right answer, or is it I who am deciding the answer in some way that I'm most comfortable with? My experience is that if I overlook this first answer, it then haunts me until I take it seriously and do something about it. Answers then come to me in the strangest ways, until I admit them to myself and do what is necessary to continue.

Transformation: I have a great and sincere desire to write. I love to write! This desire has been with me all of my life. Twenty-one years ago, one of my high school teachers smothered that dream of mine to write fiction. I was clearly told, black on white, that if I was to write then I should stick to discussion papers. I was illiterate regarding fiction. I let it happen. It became my truth.

All of these years have passed. I've worked hard to be as good as I can at writing good professional texts, while studying and later at work. I write good professional texts. I've sought the advice of competent professionals for evaluating my work. I've experienced that my thoughts and my inquiries have given me access to the resources I've needed in order to stretch myself and be as good as I can be at writing professional text. That's been my way of satisfying my inherent love of writing.

I've lived with the truth that I'm not capable of writing fiction. This fall I've worked to transform that truth in my Creative Corner, according to the four steps, and I've come out again with a new truth and a great goal. I now write fiction and master various forms of fiction. I have a story that I'm going to write in the form of a novel. I know that I write well, that my own voice is unique and good enough to communicate something to others that can give them pleasure.

**Transformation**: My truth about my self-worth. I've always been my own worst enemy. That's been a kind of defensive mechanism to avoid being hurt by others. I was prepared when it came, because I had caused it myself. In that way I created my own truth that I wasn't worth anything as a person in the eyes of others. What I did for others was what made me valuable, not my own simple existence without actions.

I've learned that my life will be no different until I learn to love myself. I can't expect others to like me if I don't like myself. I've had the knowledge for many years, but I hadn't transformed that truth that I'd had with me for so long. I didn't know that I needed to transform that truth in order to be able release it, to set it aside and go on living with a different, positive image of myself and my own self-worth.

## Hege S.

I had a toothache and made an appointment with a dentist. When I got there, the dentist said that it wasn't a toothache. The problem was that I clenched my teeth together so hard at night that it resulted in extreme pain. He said that the only solution was to use a plastic brace in my mouth at night, and I did that for only one night. After the first night I felt that wouldn't work. I felt a strong inner conviction that I could remove this myself by finding the cause and transforming it with the tools I'd learned. When I sat down and entered The Creative Corner to find the cause, I went back to thoughts about my father and the feeling that I had to be good at doing things and have accomplishments. I was at a point in my life where I didn't feel that I managed to do this. This created inner stress, so I clenched my teeth together at night and felt that I was always struggling. A part of me felt that I needed to be good at doing things for my father. When I had a conversation with him while in The Creative Corner (he is no longer alive), I had a thought that he said that he didn't care about that any more. I had a long conversation with him within me, and I was able to dissolve that old truth. I threw away the plastic brace for my teeth that day, because I was convinced that this had removed the pain. Haven't had the problem since then.

## Line

I had a difficult relationship with my father. He is an alcoholic and an artist, and often goes in and out of psychosis. I've always mothered him, while at the same time feeling bitterness and anger about things he's said or done to me.

While in The Creative Corner, I invited my father for a conversation. I asked him how we could work together to put things in order. He told me that he wanted me to be his daughter and he my father. That I shouldn't always tell him how to do or not do things in his life. He said that he missed the time when I was little and looked up to him as a father, when he could teach me things. When he said that, I had thoughts about how I could be little and he could be grown-up. We also gave each other a good hug and said that we forgave each other for what we had said and done to each other.

After that conversation I phoned him. I invited him to go to the mountains with me for a week. I asked if he could help me draw some illustrations for a website. He was *delighted*. It's been more than 20 years since I've asked him if HE could help me with something!

So we went to the mountains and had a great week. The whole time I reminded myself (in my thoughts) that I was to be a daughter and he was the father, and not to bring up things from the past that are painful, for all that is forgiven now.

I also used Nightfilms throughout that week where I envisioned each day as being extremely positive, and that's how it was too.


## *Monica*

The answer about my truth came to me while I was making dinner and was awake.

I've always felt discomfort when people raise their voices towards me. I especially remember an incident at work that was very unpleasant. I'm a nurse, and had just started working in a new hospital ward. One morning when I stood in the medicine room and was preparing medicines, my boss suddenly came in. She looked at me in a surprised way and obviously didn't like the way I had organized my work. She looked sternly at me and said in a raised voice: "We don't do it that way in this ward." She explained how things should be organized and it went well, but I had a nasty feeling inside me the rest of the day. I didn't cope well with her raised voice, and I felt stupid. For several days I was on pins and needles at work, because I was afraid that others would also shout, raise their voices or correct me.

I was standing and cutting up vegetables a few days later and it suddenly hit me: Hey, Monica, remember when you were a little girl? You were at your grandmother's. You stood downstairs in the hall and called for her. She didn't answer, so you shouted more loudly and then waited and waited. Suddenly your uncle came storming down the stairs. He was furious, grabbed you and shook you hard while he shouted: "Grandma is on the phone, this is not the way for you to behave." Then he stormed out the door, and you stood there. A little five or six year old girl. You felt stupid, afraid and unworthy.

I found out that this was my truth. I entered The Creative Corner and transformed the whole situation and the feelings I had had as a little girl. It was the same feeling that I had after the incident with my boss. When transforming it I envisioned my uncle coming down the stairs smiling. He gave me candy and put me up on his shoulders and played pony. The weather was beautiful outside, the sun was shining and everything was beautiful. He gave me a hug.

After a few days I was no longer fearful of my boss. In fact, I'm very fond of her. I'm very fond of my uncle too!

# Course participants
# tell their stories

## *Anette*

I'm sharing my story with you in hope that it can inspire others to understand how unique you all are, and that everything we need to create the life we want is already inside of us.

I'm a young woman who's had a tough start in life. Since my birth I've had to deal with a father who suffered from obsessive thoughts and a serious mental disorder. I've experienced a lot of psychological and physical abuse throughout my childhood. My mother has always been weak, and she failed to help me during times when I most needed her.

I learned very early that I had no worth and that I, as a human being, had no place here in this world. This has resulted in my attracting many bad experiences in my life, from the part of the iceberg that steers. Life became just too much for me when I was 16 years old. I suffered from depression that lasted for all of my high school years.

As an adult I've tried to think positively and make the best of life, but all the layers of traumatic experiences had caused much fear, insecurity and uncertainty in my daily life. As a result, I've never been able to really enjoy life and feel that I'm living here and now.

With a background like mine, one will often try to find some meaning in life. I've tried to find help from many self-development courses, but I must say that I felt I had been cheated.

There are a lot of self-help gurus out there who take advantage of people who are in a difficult situation. They think more about money and power than helping others. Others again feel that their way is the only right way and that there is no other truth. If your opinion differs from theirs, then they don't want to have anything to do with you.

Then there are some who mean well, but are not in balance. They think that if you're in pain and have difficulties, then you must think positive thoughts and depend on some force outside of yourself (angels, guides, goddesses, etc.) to help you.

On top of all that, you can be unlucky and come into contact with healers and clairvoyants that cause a lot of fear in people by blowing things out of proportion. They talk about ghosts and spirits that can haunt and injure you, and that there is much evil in the spirit world. These clairvoyants appear to be persons who read all your thoughts and know everything about you and your future.

By thinking positively and believing in the law of attraction I helped myself somewhat, but did not achieve great changes. I felt that in many ways I was still stuck in the same roundabouts in life. I couldn't get rid of my depression. What happened was that it finally affected my body physically, and my doctor prescribed long-term sick leave.

After a while I landed in a self-development course with Deborah, and I was very skeptical due to all my previous disappointing experiences. During that first weekend I understood that Deborah had good intentions and was an honest person. I had been afraid for a long time that Deborah would be able to read all my thoughts, and I didn't dare to talk with her. All my wrong ideas about what clairvoyance is, made me fearful.

After having been through the course with Deborah, I understood that we all carry with us some truths from earlier in life that cause us to unconsciously attract various experiences in life. Negative truths that lie buried in our subconscious don't disappear all by themselves, but they can be rewritten, so to speak. The process of changing one's truths isn't necessarily fun, but when an old truth dissolves, then old hindrances will also disappear and one will see great changes in life.

My life has been turned upside down, in a positive way. Today I can feel joy that I've longed for all my adult life. I haven't felt this way since I was 15 years old. Problems with my health have also disappeared. Since much of my "inner life" has changed, the physical conditions in my life have also changed.

Today I dare to rely on myself and my own decisions, thanks to some simple techniques that I've learned from Deborah. I no longer give my power away to others or live according to their truths. I open doors and create possibilities for myself by using my ESP sense. Talents and qualities that I didn't know I had, have gradually come forth in me as I've acquired greater inner peace.

## *Marianne*

While feeling physically exhausted and run-down—with pain, lack of sleep and inflammation in various parts of my body—I entered the classroom. I was met by a friendly pair of eyes and a smile; it was Deborah. I'd seen her on TV. I felt welcome. She walked along the rows of chairs with a look of concentration on her face, and I found a place to sit in the first row.

Seven days earlier I had received a text message from a girlfriend who wrote: "Deborah's course is something for you." She gave me the link for the website, and I read as best I could.

My health was not good. My left hand was clenched tight so often and so hard that my fingernails had twice broken in the palm of my hand. When I sat down to eat, I curled all of my toes backwards. I had to concentrate to hold my body upright due to pain—pain that I was tired of enduring—as well as lack of sleep. I pressed my tongue up against the roof of my mouth and clenched my teeth together. My neck was burning hot, so I used cold, wet towels to cool it off. Sometimes my lack of energy made it difficult to carry on a conversation for more than a few minutes. It was a great effort just to put my hand out in order to feed myself and drink liquids. I'd had trouble sleeping for a long time. I could lie awake for the whole night. Sometimes I was able to sleep a few hours, other times for just a few minutes.

It was exceptional that I had managed to get to the course that day. I had traveled by plane, train and bus without help. I also had to walk some distance from where I stayed for the course weekend to the bus, and from the bus stop to the course location. Each of these activities normally required me to wait for several hours, accumulating enough energy to be able to make a phone call, make the bed or fetch the mail, for example.

The course started. Deborah moved around and talked to the audience while radiating energy that was impossible for me to overlook. I remember that I felt happy and I admired her way of behaving. I sat there and hoped that I could get a little of what she had—it looked so good. She informed us about the weekend, and she told us that she too would have more physical energy by the end of the weekend. I was skeptical. No weekend course had ever given me more energy, and I had never heard of anyone who had taught a course for a whole weekend and ended up with more energy.

I didn't allow myself to think about the hours I would be attending the course. I had to concentrate on keeping my body upright on my chair. I also had to concentrate on concentrating; my physical pains were demanding my attention. I lost that focus very quickly, however, because Deborah captured my attention.

I was able to quickly do what Deborah said that we were to do. I was especially proud when she smilingly said, after one exercise, that it was important to remain awake during the exercises.

After that great feeling of accomplishment I found a well-deserved positive inner focus. My shoulders relaxed—this was fun. I also began to look forward to each dynamic meditation. While "in there" I experienced a pause from the painful tension in my body.

I started using what I'd learned the very first evening, and I fell asleep right away. I was astonished when I awoke to the ringing of my alarm clock the next day, and I got ready for a new course day. It felt unbelievably good to sleep for a whole night, and that was a great experience and inspiration to bring with me to the next course day.

In the afternoon of the second course day, Deborah suddenly said that there is now a lot of healing in the room. Her face was flushed, and when I looked around I saw that all of us were more or less the same.

Healing means becoming whole, Deborah said. OK, I thought, so now I'm finally going to meet someone who does healing. At the time I was willing to get up on any available healing table, but I quickly realized that this was about a different type of healing than I had thought. Deborah helped me to understand that we all have this power within us. I became both happy and proud inside. My thoughts went to my girlfriend who had recommended this course to me. Here I was, sitting and learning how to access all of the possibilities that I have within myself. It was a wonderful moment when I realized, in my own way, what Deborah was now giving me insight about and training for.

Deborah concluded the course weekend by congratulating us for completing the course, and she thanked each of us for participating. Then she put the text of a well-known Norwegian song, "I See" by Bjørn Eidsvåg on the projector screen and said that all new participants would receive their diploma after we had finished singing the song together.

She began to sing. I was overwhelmed—by her voice, the words, the tones. She sang with empathy, depth and a presence that I had never experienced before. Tears welled up in my eyes, and I let them come. They ran silently down over my cheeks in deep, deep gratitude to Deborah, and to myself. I felt that I had been met in a respectful manner and had been understood without infringement, exactly where I was in my life, on the chair in the front row. What a journey I had participated in that weekend. I was overwhelmed and happy.

I was so thankful for all that Deborah had shared with me—and with all of us at the course that weekend—from her own life. I was grateful that she had shared her insight and her knowledge with us. She had introduced us to and trained us to use techniques that we all could use to help ourselves and others around us.

It was important for me to be able to get rid of the pain, gain better health and sleep well. I knew that I now had tools that could make this possible. Another thing that made me feel very pleased, was how good it felt to become the owner of my own body and my own life.

After I proudly received my course diploma from Deborah, I walked to the bus stop. On the bus I asked myself the question: "If I had an opportunity to participate in the same course again tomorrow, would I have the strength and energy to do that?" My answer to myself was a clear "YES." I smiled to myself and thought, if the others on the bus only knew. Then I thought on an even greater scale—if the whole world only knew. My joy in life was so indescribably great; I looked forward to getting home, so I could get to work.

On the first weekend after the course I worked from morning until evening both days, establishing a new garden around my house. I lifted rocks and shoveled the earth.

I use the tools and methods that Deborah taught me every day. It's become a natural way of life.

I've had great results from attending the basic course a number of times, and I've also participated in the course that builds upon the first course I took. There have been many changes in my life, and everything is better and better for me. I'm the captain in my own life, and am now standing at the helm myself.


## Lene

I'm deeply grateful to have Deborah as my mentor. Her insight and guidance has helped me to find a magical life. Fours years ago I was an addict and abused many different substances. I've now been clean and sober since January 2007. I want to share my story and what I've learned with others, in order to help. I've contacted the police (with whom I had unfortunately already had contact) and volunteered to do things like go with them to schools and do preventive work.

On my own I've been able to help some of my old friends who didn't have an OK life. I know just how it is, and therefore I feel that I can be an inspiration.

I went to a course led by Deborah because a woman I know recommended it. I wanted to develop my abilities and become more familiar with the spiritual world. The woman said that before you do anything else, you should take a course with Deborah. I had seen her on TV, and that motivated me.

The day before my first course I got really stoned ... it turned out to be the last time for me. I had no plans to be clean after the course, but I haven't touched any drugs since that day.

When I look back upon my life as an addict, it seems like I've been in a movie. It's difficult now to look at some of the situations I've been in. Perhaps not difficult, but strange.

Today I live a happy, ordinary life, something I previously thought of as boring. I have a more comprehensive view about life and the world, and I understand that I can create my own life. It's easier for me now to understand challenges that I encounter, and I'm able to treat others that I meet with respect for their lives and their actions. I no longer interfere with what they do, but I take responsibility for my own life. Deborah has said that those who have their wits about them must use them, and I've begun to understand that I must be patient with others. They come around eventually.

When one has behaved in a way that is not acceptable for the rest of society, and in a way that is difficult to forgive, it feels good to accept that what's done is done and that I didn't know any better at that point in my life. I believe that everyone does the best they can according to where they are. If you have painful things on your conscience, you don't help yourself or anyone else by being ashamed, but by creating something new.

It's good to have admitted to myself that I'll still encounter challenges in my life. Now I have tools that I know can help me to cope. I no longer need to worry, since I know that there is a solution for everything.

My immune system has become strong and I now enjoy very good health.

Today I have a life partner, a job and smooth financial flow. I've also experienced the greatest of all; I've given birth and am mother to a handsome little boy.

The Nightfilm technique as well as transformation in The Creative Corner are nothing other than magical.

Many thanks for what you have given, and I would very much like to help you with your work.

## *Mette*

Before the course: Was seriously on my way to hitting the wall. The previous Mette was governed by destructive actions and ways of thinking.

After the course: I feel that I've found the piece that completes the puzzle (my life). I've been searching throughout my life, but there's always been something missing that I couldn't quite put my finger on. I found it, however, the weekend I participated in the course. After the course I seemed to float around in my own euphoria. I had also decided to continue this work within myself.

My life before the course was a long and painful story. I was buried in self-pity, had phobias, afflictions, illness and problems. My life was chaotic, my painful past caught up with me again and again. I had lost a lot along the way. After the course I began to work my way into the core of myself. I've recognized a lot about my life and my own problems. I still have a long way to go, but now I'm traveling on the journey with more awareness than I had earlier.

Now I can bring forth and feel the strength that I have within myself. I can enjoy the moment and the happiness within myself. I can influence my life, as opposed to how I previously let others take the helm and steer the ship (of my life) for me.

I have goals that I continuously work towards and I use my ESP sense along the way. Things come to me when I least expect them, but need them most. Coincidences happen and give me joy, inner peace and balance in life. I work my way through difficulties and challenges with the help of tools I learned to use at the course. My life that was previously so full of problems and large and small sorrows, is now full of large and small joys. My daily life and life generally flows smoothly. Life is magnificent!

I've had great progress in my life in many areas. I am more patient with myself and others. I've gotten rid of various phobias, including fear of flying. I'm better at relying on my gut feelings, and I feel more confident that I'm making the right decisions. I've taken two major exams and have used the tools while preparing for them. I was the only one in my class who received top grades on both.

I'm aware that what I focus on is what I attract. I've experienced this for better and for worse after the course. I can also say that I just "know" much more than I did earlier. I see things much more clearly now.

I could go on forever, but this is what I can recall right now.

I'm forever grateful that I "by chance" ended up taking this course. Many thanks!

## *Hege S.*

One Christmas I had no money. No money to buy gifts for my children or anything else. I was very much in despair and could see no way to solve my problems. Then I used Nightfilms to find good solutions for the whole. A short while later someone knocked on the door, and there stood a man I had been in a relationship with three years earlier. It had suddenly occurred to him that he wanted to help me, without any special reason. He was standing there with a Christmas tree and a white envelope. I thought it was a Christmas card, so I thanked him. Then he said that I should open the envelope before Christmas. I said OK, thanked him again and then closed the door. In the envelope I found a gift certificate for $1000. He receives a gift certificate from his Dad every Christmas, and it had occurred to him that he should give it to me—for some reason that he didn't understand.

The next day he called me. He'd received a phone call from his attorney saying that a dispute he'd been involved in was settled and that the damages he'd been waiting for had arrived. The amount he received was three times as much as he had given to me.

## Kari

I've worked intensely on my health since taking my first self-development course. It's been hard work, but has contributed to giving me a better life regarding health.

After having struggled with illness 24 hours a day for most of my life, I was totally worn out when I started on my first course. I had in fact worked for years on setting limits for myself, but I wasn't able to do that. Now I was thoroughly worn out, and my head was hanging towards the right side.

I was shocked when I realized what it was that had made me so sick.

All summer I've been together with a seriously ill woman, and I've taken her illness upon me. After using what I've learned, I've been able to give without absorbing her symptoms into my own body, to my delight.

After gaining so much knowledge about humans, it feels as if my life has been a psychological thriller. I've tried most everything in my 50 years of life. Then I find you and manage to heal myself. Yes, this is unbelievably powerful! Many, many thanks!

## Line tells about her daughter Henriette

After the course for teens she seemed more self-confident.

She really wants to become an actress. She's involved in a theater two days a week, and has just been to an audition for a role in a children's movie.

The day before the interview she invited Johnny Depp into The Creative Corner to get tips and advice from him for the audition. I don't know exactly what he said, but he did tell her many things that she should think about regarding facial expression and being self-confident, not nervous even when she has dyslexia.

In addition she did a Nightfilm about the audition, that it would go well (and it did).

Now she's using a Nightfilm every evening that includes a phone call telling her that she is to play that role.

Using The Creative Corner and doing a Nightfilm before the audition, helped her to avoid being nervous, and dyslexia wasn't a problem either, even though she only had five minutes to practice her lines in the manuscript.

## *May*

I've used the Nightfilm technique and The Creative Corner as support regarding a difficult claim for compensation for my daughter who was injured during childbirth. This has been a very difficult and painful process. Our claim was turned down three times. I didn't give up, but continued to work with Nightfilms and The Creative Corner. I imagined I was living in a good solution. Our case ended with the Minister of Health changing the rules and regulations so that they now include my daughter, and this will also help others in the same situation.

This case has drawn out for nine years, and that's a very long time. After I started using the tools, comprehensive solutions have appeared. The payment of damages, however, was delayed and delayed. So I thought that I needed to speed things up. I did a new Nightfilm where I "lived" that the payment arrived, and two days later the deposit was made to our account.

I know that this never would have happened if I hadn't begun to use the tools and work in this way. During the whole process I've taken deep breaths and not given up. I've used The Creative Corner to feel better myself while I've been involved in this.

I've also reached my goal about starting my own business for skin care. I used Nightfilms and The Creative Corner for this too, and imagined that I already had opened my own establishment. The result was smooth flow the whole way, and everything fell into place in the right order. The right things just came to me. Really unbelievable.

I use my ESP sense daily, and information comes to me via dreams, thoughts and ideas. Sometimes my attention is drawn to things that are in the newspaper or on the radio. Then I act on it so the smooth flow is continuous.

I really wish that everyone could learn this.


## *Raymond*

I would like to contribute my story, my truth, my gratitude to be included in Deborah's book. Without her experience, influence and tools I'd still be the same person I was earlier. I'd still be searching for the meaning of life, I'd still be depressed by all of my miscalculations and perhaps even a worse fate.

When I was five years old I found out that those who I loved as Mom and Dad, and who loved me as their child, were not in fact my parents, but were two people who had taken care of me as if I was their child since I was born.

Almost overnight I was torn away from the secure home I had known as my own, and was moved to my biological mother. My entire life was turned upside down.

My biological mother had blind faith in Jesus and discipline, she was in love with a violent and sadistic man, and she lacked experience with children; not the best combination for me.

I'll make a long story short by saying that I was neglected and lived with psychological and physical abuse for one and a half years before school and the child welfare authorities stepped in.

The case against my biological mother was closed without a court hearing since the child welfare authorities and other public authorities meant that I wasn't strong enough to cope with questioning and testifying. It was also possible that the prosecution might lose the case, enabling her to continue torturing and abusing me while I was in her legal care.

The injuries I had suffered were both physical and psychological: trauma, fear, insecurity, a blow to my self-confidence and not least discontentment with life itself.

I wanted to die already when I was seven years old. I did in fact plan suicide several times from the age of seven.

I didn't understand what the meaning of life was, what the point was in suffering so that others wouldn't be disappointed. I had to constantly find reasons to not commit suicide, and I postponed the date of my death many times before I understood that I just didn't dare to do it. There was a very likely chance that I would land in hell, since I hadn't been christened.

Back with my foster parents, in a home where they did everything they could for me, adjustment was more difficult. Their finances weren't particularly good, but I had everything I needed. The problem was that I had a need to show off, tended to be violent and was frustrated about the lack of understanding of what I was thinking. Even the child psychologist gave up because I refused to participate in two-way communication with him.

There wasn't much that changed during the next 25 years. I was the same boy, with the same attitude towards the world.

I found love for women, then lost it again, just like everyone else. When I was blessed with a child it gave me some degree of peace in my soul, something to live for, and it definitely delayed the need to end my life. I didn't, however, learn from the child how to accept life. I did my utmost to be a good father. I gave everything I had for the sake of the child, but I seldom felt joy while doing it. It was a duty.

The great change came after one of Deborah's courses. I had experienced a spiritual force, latent abilities that had appeared now and then while I was with my biological mother. Deborah has explained that Delta brainwave frequencies can "come to the surface" for people who experience traumatic episodes, and now I understand that this is the natural explanation as to why I, when a young boy, could "see" and communicate over great distances.

I had a reaction after my first course. A small one, but nonetheless a reaction. I felt I wasn't alone, that I knew, that I understood. My entire reality had been radically renewed, it was like being born again. Her tools for self-development have not only stabilized my senses, they have become the foundation upon which I could build my new life.

I'm grateful for my life. I appreciate it for the first time, and that is a new, different and wonderful feeling. I'm so grateful that I don't know how to express it.

Tears and laughter aren't enough. Today I have so much to give, because what I've received is so immeasurable. A million thanks to you, Deborah!


## *Toril*

In 2003 I hit the wall and was diagnosed as having anxiety. My symptoms became worse and worse as time went by, and I ended up isolating myself inside. It was so easy to just lie in bed and sleep. I felt secure there, for my symptoms had become so bad that I was afraid to go out and shop, was afraid to take the bus, was afraid of meeting friends, since they would then see that there was something wrong with me. I stayed far away from large shopping centers. There were always a lot of people there, and I knew that the anxiety would grip me. I thought like that every day.

A girlfriend came to me one day and said: "You know, I was at a self-development course last weekend, and you should absolutely attend. I'm sure it will help you with that anxiety of yours." I thought "OK, it can't hurt to try." Until then nothing else had helped. I registered for one of Deborah's classes.

The first course was difficult, but after getting help and advice from Deborah I decided to stay and complete the course. I didn't dare close my eyes, but Deborah looked at me and smiled while she said that I'd be trained anyway. I could go home and start changing things within myself, step by step.

I also learned how I could lower my brainwave frequency and influence others in a positive manner. I remember one time when Deborah was to demonstrate that, and she asked if anyone present had pain in their neck and shoulders. I have, I thought, but I'm not about to raise my hand. Nonetheless I found myself sitting there with my hand in the air. I saw that she looked around the room and her eyes stopped on me. Oh no, please don't ask me, I thought. I didn't dare go to the front of the room where everyone would see me. "Would you like to come up here to me?" she suddenly asked, looking at me. NO, I thought, but I heard myself saying yes. It was a strange feeling, and a scary one, as if I wasn't actually steering myself. While sitting there I thought that if there had been a hole in the floor I would have crawled into it. Everyone must see that I'm scared to death. Deborah leaned over and whispered that I just needed to relax and receive, because it was only good vibrations that would be coming. It's easy for you to say, I thought. Suddenly I felt warmth spreading in my body, and I became completely calm. Shortly thereafter she asked me to turn my head to the right and then to the left. I was able to turn my head so far that I could see over my shoulder and behind me, on both the right and the left sides. I hadn't been able to do that for many years, so I was very surprised. I must have looked like a large question mark, because she smiled and laughed afterwards.

I talked with Deborah after the class, and she recommended that I attend another class as quickly as possible. I would eventually be better, that was for sure, she said. I did as she said, and after two or three courses I was able to sit through all the exercises with my eyes closed.

I've followed up by taking additional classes when I felt I needed new inspiration. The Nightfilm technique is awesome, in addition to being able to use MY Creative Corner to transform things when I'm stuck in a rut.

Many thanks to you, Deborah, for all the support and help you've given me. I *must* say this: I had a life before the course, but oh my gosh what a life I have now. With the new insight that I have, the world looks completely different. I was completely isolated before, but now I've managed studies, I'll soon be finished with the practical experience part, and then I only have one exam left before I'll be certified to work with children and teens. I hadn't thought that would ever be possible. YIPPEE, I have a life—I'm alive!

## Gerd

Deborah, after my first course with you I've used my insight and my Creative Corner. I became a new me that weekend. I think of my life as "before" and "after" that course. I started on the journey back to MYSELF and my own power.

I've had many fantastic moments since I started that journey by turning my attention within and really started changing things within myself. Conscious energy activity is what I call it!

Becoming familiar with and deliberately using and developing my ESP sense is the smartest and most important thing I've ever done. I'd like for everyone in the whole world to understand how fantastic this insight is and what it can do in our lives, in the world, and with each and every one of us. I mean that from the bottom of my heart, even though I'm not yet healthy or free.

I use The Creative Corner and the Nightfilm technique as a lifestyle.

It's a challenge to find words to describe and explain what it in fact has meant for me, and that it has given me a different life. A complete life, where I take what happens inside of me seriously and take myself seriously. I'm on my way back to MYSELF.

Things that previously would have made me feel unhappy, frustrated or angry for weeks at a time are now taken care of in my Creative Corner, and then I'm stronger and full of new insight when I am done. I've been given tools that allow me to cope with life's ups and downs as well as various types of pain. I honestly believe that I wouldn't have been able to get through the last few years without this new knowledge. I would have been a lot worse off and suffered a lot more, I'm quite sure of that.

My new attitude is that I can learn something from everything that happens. Experiences give me an opportunity to grow and succeed down the road.

I'm on my way. Seen from the outside, my path might look somewhat unsuccessful to others, since I don't have any enormous, magical changes to refer to. Yet I've had progress, because I've really changed in many ways. My way of looking at things has definitely changed—towards what happens outside of me, around me and inside of me. How I look upon others and the world, and what that means.

I've also changed a lot physically, although I've not yet recovered from ME (*Myalgic encephalomyelitis*) and my life during recent years has been very much affected and limited by all that is happening in my body.

Since Middle school I have always had a lot of pain in my body. In the autumn of 2006 I was diagnosed as having ME and had to stop working as a file clerk. With the help of The Creative Corner technique I've been able to get rid of the worst exhaustion, but my body still behaves foolishly. The most important thing at this stage is that I've finally found and acknowledged the root cause of my challenges. Things that lie behind me and hinder my success on every level, and that is what I'm now focusing on in order to change.

I'm in an exciting, important, fantastic, but also difficult period in my life. Full of hope and trust, but also terribly frustrated and sometimes on the verge of giving up the whole process. But I don't give up. I start again. It's my turn now, because I deserve it and because I really want to beam with satisfaction about my mission in life.

I've often thought that I'm not a success story—quite the contrary—and I thought that I needed to wait until I had great physical improvement before I could share or inspire others. However, that's not true. I'm a great inspiration even though I'm not yet healthy or free. I use my tools every single day. This gives me great and magical moments, and now and then I manage to do splendid accomplishments with a lot of powerful energy. I'm also told by others who've been at the classes that I'm a fantastic inspiration and that I've had enormous progress.

I don't give up, despite great pain and some very heavy days. Those days give me great insight about myself, and I choose to use them to look forward and continue working. I choose to make the best of whatever comes along, and use my tools in order to understand here and now, and for improvements here and now. That's very important. What can I do in order to be the best I can be just now? And what do I really want?

Never give up! Just do the best you can! And to do that, The Creative Corner and the Nightfilm techniques are very helpful, and are very important for me.

No matter where you are or where you want to be, it's terrific to go to an ESP course, learn techniques and get new insight that improves your life. I don't know how I'd have gotten through these years that are now behind me, without them. My conscious energy activity and my new life started with you and your course, Deborah.

I intend to continue looking for success and focusing on the best that I can do, and before you and I know it, my story will have changed to a really marvelous success story, visible for all that I am radiantly active, super healthy, free, and full of my own unique power.

Some people change themselves in the blink of an eye, and some need more patience and time. In the meantime I'm doing my very best and I'm looking towards all that is good. Even if life isn't easy, one can still do one's best and feel well off exactly where one is here and now.

The happy moments appear suddenly, at the strangest times and in the strangest ways, so keep your eyes open and welcome them. The ESP course has definitely opened me for happiness at a completely different level than before.

Many, many, many thanks so far. I'm really looking forward to the sequel. Huge hug!

### Gunn

Dear Unique Mind ESP. I would like to share a moving and true story that may give hope and help to others.

"Tore" came to our family after having been examined at a psychiatric institution for children and youth. The reason for this examination was that he had taken complete control at home, dominating his Mom and his younger siblings. He'd not gone to school for 75 percent of the school year. His Mom had completely lost control of him in every way, and became physically ill due to the situation.

Quote from his journal: "Diagnosis: Unspecified radical disturbance of development. Specific development disturbance in motor proficiency. Considerable and widespread social disturbance. ADI (Autism Diagnostic Interview): 'Tore' scores under the cutoff for autism in all areas (that is, repeated behavior and stereotype patterns). It is obvious that 'Tore' has difficulty with social interaction. He has been described as being stubborn and dominating, and wants everything to happen on his terms. Examinations reveal autism-like social inhibition that is similar to Asperger's syndrome. His family and others around him will probably need professional guidance."

That summer the situation was completely at an impasse, and he came to live with us. The intention was originally for him to stay here until the child welfare authorities found a place for him in an institution, which he refused. It was therefore decided that he could stay with us, provided that he attended school. If that didn't work, he'd need to go to an institution.

He'd spent the past year at home on the sofa, doing nothing but watch TV and play computer games. He had no routines at all. Everything had to be learned anew: personal hygiene like showering, brushing teeth and changing clothes as well as eating regular meals, eating with a knife and fork, going to school, social relations, etc. The only things he ate were hot dogs and pizza, and he had to "learn" to eat sandwiches, potatoes and the like. It was a long process for all of us.

We have two children, one who is older and one younger than "Tore," and they welcomed him in a fantastic manner. They've never said a bad word to him and have supported him in every manner. This is unusual in homes with foster children, as conflicts often arise.

I took my first course in May 2004, and in September that year I repeated the course. While in one of the meditation exercises in September I received a very clear message: You are to work with youth and courses. I wasn't able to interpret this at the time, and thought about it for several days. The message was so clear, but I didn't understand. I had a job and hadn't thought of changing jobs either. I felt I had enough to do in the situation we were already in.

I called Deborah after a few days, because I HAD to get an answer. She wasn't hiring, so she advised me to use one of the techniques and ask what this message meant for me. It took a long time before I understood that it was "Tore" that I was to work with.

I used EVERYTHING I had learned at the courses in order to help get him going in a better direction. Progress was slow but sure. He went to school every day, and we managed to introduce routines again, one after another. He often made comments about how surprised he was at what I was able to get him to do. "Are you a magician or something?" he would often ask.

The following May, the professional team that had given him a psychiatric examination was so surprised by his progress that they asked for a meeting with his school and our family. They wanted to find the key to his great progress. It's very rare that children who are in as bad a state as he had been make so much progress, they commented. His condition had been so poor that they had feared for his life. His mom also says that she doubts that he would be alive today if he had continued to live at home. At the meeting with the school, they were asked what they had done to accomplish this. They answered that they had given the class some extra resources that were divided among all of the students, as there were several in the class that needed extra help. No one had therefore noticed anything special about "Tore." One of the professionals put their hands to their head and said: *it's not possible!*

After "Tore" finished high school he moved to a place of his own and started studying, but soon gave that up. He was unsure of the choice he had made and wanted to work while he was considering what direction to go in. He presently works in a restaurant kitchen and likes that. He wants to work for another year before studying again.

He's also expanded his social network, and takes the initiative to contact friends, something he never did earlier.

Today he appears to be an attractive young man, and it's difficult to see that there is anything different about him. When he came to us it was easy to see that something was seriously wrong. It was very obvious from his behavior and his way of communicating with others. He is living evidence that the insight the course has taught us to use, really works. I would also like to add that he hasn't had any professional help along the way. "Tore" hasn't had professional help after his first examination. I've only used the tools I learned at the course. He's getting along well in every way, and I'm not worried about his future.

Great thanks and a hug from Gunn.

# *Afterword*

> "When you become familiar with yourself, you will never need to be afraid of being revealed."
>
> —Deborah Borgen

My vision in life is peace on earth. Many people say: "Deborah you're dreaming." Yes, and I am so happy that I have the ability to dream because that is actually the first step. I believe that we can create peace, but it starts within each of us.

I have started there, within myself. I used to say: If I can find peace within me then everyone can. This was important for me to prove scientifically, and I've done so.

The result reveals a great leap within mind development for a more sustainable and effective use of one's own brain. In my words, it says: Now we can all use our minds in this way and create peace.

Here some of the results from the research. More information is available at www.uniquemind.org.

Excerpt from research report with questionnaire:

- Change in intuition is the strongest and most consistent change that was measured after the course. The change is both statistically and clinically significant, with an effect of over 0.8 (Cohen's d). When it comes to questionnaires, participants may sometimes answer in a way that they believe the researchers and others want them to answer. It is, however, not possible to change one's measured brainwave activity to satisfy researchers in this way. Seen together, it is likely that participants have experienced an increase in use and capacity for intuition that has a noticeable effect in daily life.

- A statistically and clinically significant increase in feelings of mastering, were registered when considering all participants together. The increase is moderate, but participants can most likely notice this change in their lives.

- A statistically and clinically significant increase in satisfaction with life was found when measured using the Satisfaction With Life Scale. The increase may be considered mild to moderate. In addition, a statistically significant increase in the sum score of our ad hoc questions about satisfaction with specific areas of life was found ($p = 0.001$). This increase has a moderate to high effect size of 0.70 (Cohen's d). This indicates an increase that should be noticeable for participants.

- Significant changes in the presence of meaning in life was found. The effect may be considered mild to moderate; how much this influences the participants in their lives is not known. The difference may nonetheless be considered clinically significant, with an effect size of 0.36 (Cohen's d). The fact that the changes are also seen in measureable changes in brain activity supports the reliability of this finding of increased meaning in life.

- A statistically and clinically significant improvement of depressive symptoms was found after the course. Changes in depressive symptoms as measured with CES-D correlates highly with our measurement of psychosomatic symptoms of depression. This supports the reliability of both scales. As expected, the improvement of depressive symptoms correlates negatively with changes in feelings of mastering. It also seems that changes in use of intuitive thinking is related to improvement of depression. An explanation may be that use of intuition or an experiential system leads to less brooding. Overall, there is reason to believe that most participants have experienced significant improvement of depressive symptoms.

- Participants reported significant ($p > 0.001$) increase of mystical experiences after the course. Changes have a moderate effect size (0.42). This is likely to affect the perceived experience of the participants. A correlation was also found between an increase in mystical experiences and an increase of intuitive and rational thinking. The score on mystical experiences at time 2 correlates with use of the "Nightfilm" technique. Taken together, an interpretation may be that magical experiences play a significant role in the processes of change.

It is my hope that I have motivated and encouraged you through this book to start with your deliberate development, and I wish you the best of luck!

*Blessings from Deborah*

# About the authors

## Deborah Borgen

Deborah Borgen was born in Canada, but grew up in Oslo, Norway. She studied economics and marketing at the BI Norwegian School of Management and has worked as a business manager in the construction industry.

Deborah has worked with self-development since 1986. She has been an instructor for The Silva Method and Silva UltraMind ESP Systems. In January 2010, after 24 years of research and development, Deborah presented her own new program: "From gut feeling to goal-oriented self-development." She is the founder and leader of Unique Mind ESP, a company that aims to spread this program to people throughout the world. Deborah is well-known in Norway from several Norwegian TV-series. She has also worked with professional aspects of an international TV series.

## Kim Bjørnqvist

Kim Bjørnqvist has his background in advertising. For the past 12 years he has worked on developing ideas for TV series in two of Norway's largest production companies. Kim has previously written two books, both in Norwegian. He is now self-employed as a consultant for advertising and TV. He also lectures for businesses and serves as a guest lecturer at several film schools outside of his home country of Norway.